James Runciman

The Romance of the Coast

James Runciman

The Romance of the Coast

ISBN/EAN: 9783744679374

Printed in Europe, USA, Canada, Australia, Japan

Cover: Foto ©Thomas Meinert / pixelio.de

More available books at **www.hansebooks.com**

THE ROMANCE OF THE COAST.

THE ROMANCE OF THE COAST.

BY

JAMES RUNCIMAN.

LONDON: GEORGE BELL AND SONS,
YORK STREET, COVENT GARDEN.
1883.

CHISWICK PRESS:—C. WHITTINGHAM AND CO., TOOKS COURT,
CHANCERY LANE.

TO FREDERICK GREENWOOD,

EDITOR OF THE *St. James's Gazette.*

DEAR SIR,

I dedicate this little book to you. When you first gave me the chance of escaping from the unkindly work of political journalism, I used to think that your treatment of efforts which I thought extremely fine, was somewhat heartless. I am glad now that I have passed under your severe discipline, and I am proud to be one of the school of writers whose professional success is due to your help and training.

I am, Dear Sir,

Yours very faithfully,

JAMES RUNCIMAN.

CONTENTS.

viii CONTENTS.

THE ROMANCE OF THE COAST.

AN OLD-SCHOOL PILOT.

A T the mouth of a north-country river a colony of
pilots dwelt. The men and women of this colony
looked differently and spoke a dialect different from
that used by the country people only half a mile off.
The names, too, of the pilot community were different
from those of the surrounding population. Tully was
the most common surname of all, and the great
number of people who bore it were mostly black-eyed
and dark-haired, quite unlike our fair and blue-eyed
north-country folk. Antiquaries say the Romans
must have lived on the spot for at least two hundred
years, judging by the coins and the vast quantities of
household materials unearthed ; and so some persons
have no difficulty in accounting for the peculiarities of
the pilot colony. Speculations of this sort are, however, somewhat beside the mark. It is only certain
that the pilots lived amongst themselves, intermarried,
and kept their habits and dialect quite distinct. When
a pilot crossed the line a hundred yards west of his
house, he met people who knew him by his tongue to
be a "foreigner."

My particular friend among the pilots was a very

B

big man, who used to amuse us much by the childish gravity of his remarks. He was a remnant of a past generation, and the introduction of steam shocked his faculties beyond recovery. He would say : " In the old times, sir, vessels had to turn up here. It was back, fill, and shiver-r-r all the way; but now you might as well have sets of rails laid on the water and run the ships on them. There is no seamanship needed." He never quite forgave the Commissioners for deepening the river. As he said in his trenchant manner : " There used to be some credit in bringing a ship across the bar when you were never quite sure whether she would touch or not ; but now you could bring the ' Duke of Wellington ' in at low water. These kid-gloved captains come right up to their moorings as safe as if they were driving a coach along the road." He was quite intolerant of railways, too ; but then his first experience of the locomotive engine was not pleasant. Somehow he got on to the railway line on a hazy night ; and just as the train had slowed down to enter the station the engine struck him and knocked him over. The engine-driver became aware of a brief burst of strong language, and in great alarm called upon two porters to walk along the line to see what had happened. They did so of course, and when they got to the place of the accident the light of their lanterns revealed the pilot perfectly sound and engaged in brushing dirt off his clothes. When he saw the bright buttons of the railway officials the thought of the police came instantly into his mind, and he said, " Here, now, you needn't be taking me up ; if I've done any damage to your engine I'll pay for it." At another time he was bringing a ship northwards when he was invited by the captain to run down below and help himself to a nip of brandy. After taking his brandy he proceeded to light his pipe at the stove. Now the captain possessed a large monkey, and the creature was shivering near the fire. The pilot said, " A gurly day, sir ; " and the monkey gave a responsive shiver. The pilot went on with affable gruffness, " The Soutar light's away on the port bow now, sir; " and still the monkey made no answer. Not to be stalled off, the pilot proceeded, " We'll be over the bar in an hour, sir." But failing to elicit a response even to this pleasant information, he stepped up on deck, and ranging himself alongside of the captain on the bridge, said, " What a quiet chap your father is ! "

The first time I saw my poor friend I liked him. We lived in a lonely house that stood on the cliffs at a bleak turn of the coast. One wild morning a coble beat into our cove. It looked as though the sea must double on her every second ; but just when the combers shot at her most dangerously the man at the tiller placed the broad square stern at right angles to the path of the travelling wave, and she lunged forward safely. By dexterous jockeying she was brought close in, and the men came through the shallow water in their sea-boots. They were blue with cold, and begged for a little tea or coffee. Hot cakes and coffee happened to be just ready; so the fellows had a hearty breakfast and went away. With prolonged clumsiness the pilot shook the hand of the lady who had entertained him ; and in two days after the boat sailed into the cove again amid nasty weather, and the master came ashore with a set of gaudy wooden bowls painted black and red. These he solemnly presented to the lady of the house. He had run thirty miles against a northerly sea to bring them.

When I next saw the pilot he had fallen upon very hard times. The system of keeping " privileged men" had obtained great hold in the north. The privileged pilot does not need to go out and beat about at sea in search of vessels; he can lie comfortably in his bed until he is signalled, and then he steps aboard without any of the trouble of competition. However good this system may be in a general way, it bears very hardly on the poor fellows who have to lie off for two or three days together on the chance of getting a ship. We were passing by Flamborough Head in a large steamer when the mate came down below and said, "There is a pilot-boat from our town astern there, sir." The captain shouted, "Tell them to stop her directly and take the coble in tow." We then blew our whistle, and the pilot-boat drew up alongside. My friend stepped aboard, and the captain said, " Come away down and have some breakfast." The pilot tried to speak, but his voice broke. He said : "No, I can't eat. When you passed us, we baith started to cry ; and when you whistled for us, maw heart com' oot on its place, an' it'll gan back ne mair." The poor men had had no food for two days. In spite of his tragic statement, the pilot recovered, and ate a very good breakfast indeed ; and his boat towed astern of us till he placed us at our moorings.

He met his end like a brave man in the great October gale which all of us remember. He was down on the pier smoking with his friends in the watch-house and looking out occasionally for distressed vessels. The great seas were hurling themselves over the stone-work and shattering into wild wreaths of foam on the sand. Strong men who showed them-selves outside full in the face of the wind were blown down flat as if they had been tottering children. The wind sounded as though it were blown through a huge trumpet, and the sea was running nine feet on the bar. A small vessel fought through, and appeared likely to get into the fair-way. She showed her port light for a time, and all seemed going well. Suddenly she opened both her red and her green lights, and it was seen that she was coming dead on for the pier. Presently she struck hard, within thirty yards of the stone-work. There was wild excitement amongst the brigade men, for they saw that she must be smashed into matchwood in five minutes. The rockets were got ready ; but before a shot could be fired the ill-fated vessel gave way totally. A great sea rushed along the side of the pier, and the pilot saw something black amongst the travelling water. " There's a man ! " he shouted; and without a moment's thought plunged in, calling on the other fellows to pitch him a rope. Had he tied a line around his waist before he jumped he would have been all right. As it was, the Dutchman whom he tried to save was washed clean on to the pier and put safely to bed in the brigade-house. The pilot was not found until two days afterwards.

AN UGLY CONTRAST.

THE steam-tug "Alice," laden with excursionists from several Tyneside towns, struck in the autumn of 1882 on the Bondicar Rocks, sixteen miles north of Blyth. The boat was not much damaged, and could easily have been run into the Coquet River within a very few minutes if the passengers had only kept steady. But the modern English spirit came upon the men, and a rush was made for the boat. Women and children were hustled aside; and the captain of the tug had to threaten certain persons of his own sex with violence before he could keep the crowd back. Some twenty-seven people clambered into the boat, and then a man of genius cut away the head-rope, and flung the helpless screaming company into the sea. Twenty-five of them were drowned. It will be a relief if time reveals any ground of hope that the men of our manufacturing towns will lose no more of the virtues which we used to think a part of the English character—coolness and steadiness and unselfishness in times of danger, for example. The Englishmen who live in quiet places have not become cowardly, so far as is ascertained; nor are they liable to womanish panic. In the dales and in the fishing-villages along our north-east coast may still be found plenty of brave men. Where such disgraceful scenes as that rush to the "Alice's" boat are witnessed, or selfishness like that of the men who got away in the boats of the "Northfleet," there we generally find that the civilization of towns has proved fatal to coolness and courage.

Curiously enough, it happens that within six miles of the rock where the "Alice" struck, a splendidly brave thing was done, which serves in itself to illustrate the difference that is growing up between the race that lives by the factory and the men who earn their bread out-of-doors. Passing southward from the Bondicar Rocks you come to a shallow stream that sprawls over the sand and ripples into the sea. You wade this stream, and walk still southward by the side of rolling sand-hills. The wind hurls through the hollows, and the bents shine like grey armour on the bluffs of the low heights. You are not likely to meet any one on your way, not even a tramp. Presently the hills open, and you come to the prettiest village on the whole coast. The green common slopes down to the sea, and great woods rustle and look glad all round the margin of the luxuriant grass-land. Along the cliff straggle a few stone houses, and the square tower with its sinister arrow-holes dominates the row. There is smooth water inshore ; but half a mile or so out eastward there runs a low range of rocks. One night a terrible storm broke on the coast. The sea rose, and beat so furiously on the shore that the spray flew over the Fisher Row, and yellow sea-foam was blown in patches over the fields. The waters beyond the shore were all in a white turmoil, save where, far off, the grey clouds laid their shoulders to the sea and threw down leaden shadows. Most of the ships had gone south about; but one little brig got stuck hard-and-fast on the ledge of rocks that runs below the village. She had eight men aboard of her, and these had to take to the rigging; where the people on shore heard them shouting. It is a fearful kind of noise, the crying of men in a wrecked ship. Morning broke, and the weather was wilder than ever. There was no life-boat in the place, and it was plain that the vessel could not stand the rage of the breakers much longer. It was hard to see the ship at all, the spray came in so thickly. The women were crying and wringing their hands on the bank; but that was of small avail. However, one little trouting-boat lay handy, and her owner determined to go off in her to the brig. He was a fine fellow to look at—quite a remarkable specimen of a man, indeed. Without any flurry, without a sign of emotion on his face, he said, " Who's coming? " His two sons stepped out, and the boat was moved towards the water's edge.

Just then a carter came down to look at the wreck. The carter's mare was terror-stricken by the wrath of the sea, and galloped down the beach. In passing the coble the mare plunged, and the axle-tree of the cart staved in the head of the boat below the water-line. This was very bad; but the leader of the forlorn hope did not give himself time to waver. Taking off his coat, he stuffed it into the hole; and then, calling in another volunteer, he said, " Sit against that." The men took their places very coolly, and the little boat was thrust out amid the broken water. Amidst all this the face of one woman who stood looking at the men arrested my attention. It was very white, and her eyes had a look in them that I cannot describe, though I have seen it since in my sleep. The men in the boat were her husband and her sons. She said nothing, but kept her hands tightly clasped; and her lips parted every time the boat rose on the crown of a wave. We could not see those good fellows half the time : all we could tell was that the man who was sitting against the jacket had to bale very hard. Presently the deep bow of the boat rose over a travelling sea, and she ground on the sand. She was heavily laden with the brig's crew of limp and shivering Danish seamen. And it was not a moment too soon for her to be ashore : the brig parted almost directly, and the wreckage was strewn all along the beach.

The men who did this action never had any reward. And it did not matter ; for they took a very moderate view of their own merits. They knew, of course, that they had done a good morning's work ; but it never occurred to them that they ought to have a paragraph in the newspapers and be called brave. The sort of courage they exhibited they would have described, if their attention had been called to it, as " only natural." The old hero who went through a heavy sea with a staved-in boat is still living. His name is Big Tom, and his home is at Cresswell, in the county of Northumberland. He does not know that he is at all heroic ; but it is pleasant to think of him after reading about those wretched excursionists who drowned each other in sheer fright within sight of his home. He has often saved life since then. But when he puts out to sea now he does not need to use a stove-in coble: he is captain of the smart lifeboat; and his proudest possession is a photograph which shows his noble figure standing at the bow.

THE FISHERWOMAN.

ON bleak mornings you might see the movements
of Peggy's stooping figure among the glistening
brown weeds that draped the low rocks; and somehow
you always noticed her most on bleak mornings.
When the joy of the summer was in the air, and the
larks were singing high up in the sky, it seemed rather
pleasant than otherwise to paddle about among the
quiet pools and on the cold bladder-wrack. But when
the sky was leaden, and the wind rolled with strange
sounds down the chill hollows, it was rather pitiful to
see a barefooted woman tramping in those bitter places.
The sea seemed to wait for every fresh lash of the
blast; and when the grey water sprang into brief
spurts of spray you felt how cruelly Peggy's bare
limbs were cut by the wind. But she took it all
kindly, and made no moan about anything. Towards
eight o'clock you would meet her tramping over the
sand with her great creel full of bait slung on her
forehead. Her feet gripped at the sand, and her
strong leg looked ruddy and hard. Her hands were
always rough, and covered with little scratches
received while she baited the lines; but these were no
miseries to Peggy, and her face always seemed composed and quiet. She would not pass you without a

word, and her voice was pleasant with low gutturals. If her eyes reminded you of the sea, you put it down to a natural fancy. They were not at all poetic or sentimental; for Peggy was a rough woman. But something there was in the gleam of her pale clear eyes that made you think of the far northern seas, by the borders of which her forefathers in a remote time were probably born. As I have said, Peggy could use very rough words when farmers' wives tired her with too much chaffering; but mostly her face had a hard placidity that refreshed the mind, just as it is refreshed by considering the deliberate ways of harmless animals.

Towards eleven in the morning Peggy would be seated in her warm kitchen, beside a flat basket in which mysterious coils of brown twine wound round and round. The brown twine had tied to it long lines of horse-hair snoods with sharp white hooks lashed on by slips of waxed thread. Peggy baited one after another of these hooks and laid them dexterously so that the line might be shot overboard without entanglement. You might sit down in the sanded kitchen to talk to the good woman if you were not nice about fishy odours. If you led on to such subjects, she would bring out her store of ghostly stories : how a dead lady walked in the shrubberies by the tower after the squire's sons murdered her lover; and how the old clock in the tower had a queer light travelling over its face on one day of the year. Or she would gossip about the folks in the place; telling you how poor Jemmy had lost money, and how old Adam had got a rare stocking, and him meeting the priest every day like a poor man. You might smoke as much as you liked in Peggy's kitchen ; and for various reasons it was just as well to keep smoking : the sanitary principles of Dr. Richardson are not known in the villages on the coast. Peggy herself did not smoke, because it was not considered right for women to use tobacco until they were past the age of sixty-five. After that they had their weekly allowance with the groceries. In the evenings of bright days you saw Peggy at her best. When the dusk fell, and the level sands shone with a deep smooth gloss, you would see strange figures bowing with rhythmic motions. These figures were those of women. All the women of the village turn out on the sand to hunt for sand-eels. To catch a sand-eel requires long practice. You take two iron hooks, and work them down deep in the sand when the tide has just gone. With quick but steady movements, you make a series of deep " criss-crosses ;" and when the fish is disturbed by the hooks you whip him smartly out, and put him in the basket before his magical wriggle has taken him deep into the sand again. The women stooping over the shining floor look like ghostly harvesters reaping invisible crops. They are very silent, and their steps are feline. Peggy worked out her day, and then she would go home and cut up the eels for the next day's lines. In the early morning the men came in, and then Peggy had to turn out and carry the fish to the cart that drove inland to the coach or the railway station. It was not a gay life ; but still each fresh day brought the lads and their father home, and Peggy could not have looked at them, and more especially perhaps at her great sons, without being proud of her men-folk. While they were sleeping she had to be at work, so that the home life was restricted, but it was abundantly clear that in a rough and silent way the whole of the family were fond of each other; and if Peggy could spare little more than a glance when the brown sail of the coble came in sight, it is probable that she felt just as much as ladies who have time for long and yearning looks.

There came a time when Peggy needed no more to look out for the sail. Her husband went stolidly down to the boat one evening, and her three sons followed with their weighty tread. The father was a big, rugged man with a dark face ; the lads were yellow-haired, taking after their mother. Some of the fishermen did not like the look of the evening sky, but Peggy's husband never much heeded the weather.

Next day the wind came away very strong, and the cobles had to cower southward under a bare strip of mainsail. The men ashore did not like to be asked whether they thought the weather would get worse ; and the women stood anxiously at their doors. A little later and they gathered all together on the rock-edge. One coble, finely handled, was working steadily up to the bend where the boats ran in for the smooth water, and Peggy followed every yard that the little craft gained. All the world for her depended on the chance of weathering that perilous turn. The sail was hardly to be seen for the drift that was plucked off the crests of the waves. Too soon Peggy saw a great roller double over and fold itself heavily into the boat. Then there was the long wallowing lurch, and the rudder came up, while the mast and the sodden sail went under. It is bad enough for a woman to read in some cold official list about the death of her father, her husband, her son; but very much worse it is for the woman who sees her dearest drowning— standing safe ashore to watch every hopeless struggle for life. One of the fishers said to Peggy, " Come thy ways in, my woman; and we'll away and seek them." But Peggy walked fast across the sand and down to the place where she knew the set of the tide would carry the dead lads in. The father came first ashore. She wiped the froth from his lips and closed his eyes, and then hastened further northward where her eldest son was flung on the beach. Peggy saw in an instant that his face was bruised, and moaned at the sight of the bruises; his father looked as though he were sleeping. The other lads did not come ashore till next day, and Peggy would not go home all the night through. In the dark she got away from the kind fellows who stayed by her; and when they sought her she was kneeling in the hollow of a sand- hill where another of her boys lay—her face pressed against the grass.

These bold fellows were laid in the ground, and next day Peggy started silently to work. The grandfather —that is, her husband's father, an old man, quite broken by the loss of his son—was brought home to his son's fireside, where the two may be seen to-day: their thoughts divided between their dead and the business of getting bread for to-morrow.

THE VETERAN.

IN the mornings a chair used to be placed on the
cliff-side facing the sea, and towards ten o'clock a
very old man would walk slowly down the village street
and take his seat. A little shelf held his pipe and
tobacco-jar, and he would sit and smoke contentedly
until the afternoon. The children used to play around
him with perfect confidence, although he seldom spoke
to them. His face looked as if it were roughly carved out
of stone, and his complexion was of a deep rich brown.
On his watch-chain he wore several trinkets, and he was
specially proud of one thin disk: this was the Nile
medal; for the old man had been in the fight at
Aboukir. He seldom spoke about his experience of
life on board a man-of-war; he was far more interested
in bestowing appreciative criticism on the little coasters
that flitted past northward and southward, and in saying
severe things about the large screw colliers. But
although he had little to tell about his fighting experiences, he was a hero none the less. He lived in a
little white cottage at the high end of the Green, and
a woman came every morning to attend to his simple
wants; for his old wife had died long ago. He was
lonely, and not much noticed outside the village; yet

he had done, in his time, one of the finest things known in the history of bravery.

The Veteran lived happily in his way. He had made some money in a small sloop with which he used to run round to the Firth; good things were sent to him from the Hall; and the head gardener had orders to let him have whatever fruit and vegetables he wanted. He had no wish to see populous places: his uneventful life was varied enough for his desires. If he were properly coaxed, he was willing to tell many things about Nelson; but, strange to say, he was not fond of the great Admiral. Collingwood was his man, and he always spoke with reverence about the north-country sailor. He cared very little for glory; and he estimated men on the simple principle that one kind man is worth twenty clever ones and a hundred plucky ones. The story of his acquaintance with Collingwood and Nelson was strange. In 1797 the Veteran was just nineteen years old; but he had already got command of a little sloop that plied up the Firth, and he was accounted one of the best sailors on the coast. His father was a hearty man of eight-and-forty, and had retired from the sea.

Now it happened that the wealthiest shipowner of the little port had a very wild and unsteady son, who was a ship captain and sailed one of his father's vessels. The shipowner was anxious to see some steady man sail with his lad; so he asked the Veteran's father to go as mate of a barque which the son was going to take out to Genoa. The terms offered were so very tempting that the old man decided to take another short spell of the sea; and when the Veteran

next brought his little sloop on to the Hard, he found
his father had run round to Hull in the barque.   The
young captain, of whom the old man had taken charge,
behaved very badly during the southerly trip, and in
the end had delirium tremens.   During the whole of
the night the madman divided his time between giving
contradictory orders and crying out with fear of the
dreadful things which he said were chasing him.   On
the night after the vessel brought up at Hull he
staggered aboard, and stumbled into the cabin.
Sitting down at the table, he set himself deliberately
to insult his mate, who had been quietly reading.   He
called the old man a pig, and asked him why he had
not gone to his sty.   Finding that all his insults were
received with good humour, he grew bolder, and at
last went round the table and hit out heavily.   A
white mark appeared on the mate's cheek where the
blow landed, and in return he delivered a tremendous
right-hander full in the captain's face.   The bully was
lifted off his feet and fell against the cabin-door, crashing one of the panels out.   He rose, wiped the blood
from his mouth, and went ashore.

The lieutenant of a frigate which was lying in the
harbour was ashore with a press-gang.   The drunkard
went and declared that the Veteran's father had been
insubordinate, and showed a bruised face in evidence.
So in the grey of the morning the naval officer and
half-a-dozen seamen came under the barque's quarter
and climbed aboard.   The old man was walking the
deck, being very much perturbed about the last night's
affray, and he grasped the whole situation at once.
He picked up a handspike and got ready to defend

himself; but the seamen made a rush, and a blow with the flat of a heavy cutlass knocked the old sailor senseless. When he came to himself he found that he was on board the guardship.

Two days after the Veteran was strolling along the quay in all the glory of white duck and blue pilot cloth. (Sailors were great dandies in those days, and every one of the little ports from the Firth to the Foreland had its own particular fashion in the matter of go-ashore rig.) The Veteran was going to be married as soon as his next trip was over; and on this particular evening he intended to stroll through the lanes and see his sweetheart, who was a farmer's daughter. A fine southerly breeze was blowing, and a little fishing smack crossed the bar and ran up the harbour, lying hard over with press of sail. The Veteran had the curiosity to wait until the little craft had brought up, and he watched the dingey come ashore with two men aboard. He was very much surprised to hear one of the men mention his name; so he turned to ask what was wanted. The fisherman handed him a dirty letter, and on opening it the Veteran found that it was from one of the able seamen aboard the barque. The writer briefly told the circumstances, and then added that there would be no delivery from the guardship for four days. Within two hours the smack was beating away to the southward with the Veteran in her. He had bidden his sweetheart good-bye, telling her quietly that they could not be married for a long time; but she did not know then how very long it would be.

The Veteran helped to work the smack round to the

Humber, and it is probable that his thoughts during the trip were not cheerful. He had asked a friend to take charge of his sloop, and had rapidly countermanded all the preparations that were being made for his marriage. On arriving at Hull the Veteran went at once on board the guardship, and was shown into the commander's cabin. His business was soon over, and a sergeant of marines took him down to the wretched cockpit, where he found his father lying with cloths about his head. The lad said quite simply, " I want you to go ashore, father, and look after the girl until I come back; I have volunteered in your stead." The old man would have liked to argue the point; but he knew that his son would not give way, and so he submitted.

Long afterwards the Veteran used to tell us that that was one of the best moments of his life, although his heart had been so heavy at going away from home. So the young sailor joined the "Minotaur" and fought at the Nile. He was many years at sea; and before he got back to the town he had risen to be sailing-master of a forty-four. When he came to be married, all the little vessels in the harbour made themselves gay with their colours, and the church bells were rung for him as though he had been a great personage.

He lived long enough for his brief story to be forgotten; and only the clergyman and the squire, among all the people of the village where he died, knew that the old man was in the least a hero. They knew that he was fond of children, and they were all willing to run to oblige him. Perhaps he wanted no better reward. In these days of advertisement, much would have been made of him ; for the great Collingwood had specially mentioned him for a brilliant act of bravery. As it was, he got very little pension and no fame.

THE HEROINE OF A FISHING VILLAGE.

UNTIL she was nineteen years old, Dorothy lived a very uneventful life; for one week was much the same as another in the placid existence of the village. On Sunday mornings, when the church-bells began to ring, you would meet her walking over the moor with a springy step. Her shawl was gay, and her dress was of the most pronounced colour that could be bought in the market-town. Her brown hair was gathered in a net, and her calm eyes looked from under an old-fashioned bonnet of straw. Her feet were always bare, but she carried her shoes and stockings slung over her shoulder. When she got near the church she sat down in the shade of a hedge and put them on; then she walked the rest of the distance with a cramped and civilized gait. On the Monday mornings early she carried the water from the well. Her great "skeel" was poised easily on her head; and, as she strode along singing lightly without shaking a drop of water over the edge of her pail, you could see how she had come by her erect carriage. When the boats came in, she went to the beach and helped to carry the baskets of fish to the cart. She was then dressed in a sort of thick flannel blouse and a singular quantity of brief petticoats. Her head was bare, and she looked far better than in her Sunday clothes.   If the morning were fine she sat out in the sun and baited the lines, all the while lilting old country songs in her guttural dialect.   In the evening she would spend some time chatting with other lasses in the Row; but she never had a very long spell of that pastime, for she had to be at work winter and summer by about five or six in the morning.   The fisher-folk do not waste many candles by keeping late hours.   She was very healthy and powerful, very ignorant, and very modest.   Had she lived by one of the big harbours, where fleets of boats come in, she might have been as rough and brazen as the girls often are in those places.   But in her secluded little village the ways of the people were old-fashioned and decorous, and girls were very restrained in their manners.   No one would have taken her to be anything more than an ordinary country girl had not a chance enabled her to show herself full of bravery and resource.

Every boat in the village went away North one evening, and not a man remained in the Row excepting three very old fellows, who were long past work of any kind.   When a fisherman grows helpless with age he is kept by his own people, and his days are passed in quietly smoking on the kitchen settle or in looking dimly out over the sea from the bench at the door.   But a man must be sorely " failed " before he is reduced to idleness, and able to do nothing that needs strength.   A southerly gale, with a southerly sea, came away in the night, and the boats could not beat down from the northward. By daylight they were all safe in a harbour about eighteen miles north of the village. The sea grew worse and worse, till the usual clouds of foam flew against the houses or skimmed away into the fields beyond. When the wind reached its height the sounds it made in the hollows were like distant firing of small-arms, and the waves in the hollow rocks seemed to shake the ground over the cliffs. A little schooner came round the point, running before the sea. She might have got clear away, because it was easy enough for her, had she clawed a short way out, risking the beam sea, to have made the harbour where the fishers were. But the skipper kept her close in, and presently she struck on a long tongue of rocks that trended far out eastward. The tops of her masts seemed nearly to meet, so it appeared as if she had broken her back. The seas flew sheer over her, and the men had to climb into the rigging. All the women were watching and waiting to see her go to pieces. There was no chance of getting a boat out, so the helpless villagers waited to see the men drown; and the women cried in their shrill, piteous manner. Dorothy said, " Will she break up in an hour? If I thowt she could hing there, I would be away for the lifeboat." But the old men said, " You can never cross the burn." Four miles south, behind the point, there was a village where a lifeboat was kept; but just halfway a stream ran into the sea, and across this stream there was only a plank bridge. Half a mile below the bridge the water spread far over the broad sand and became very shallow and wide. Dorothy spoke no more, except to say " I'll away." She ran across the moor for a mile, and then scrambled down to the sand so that the tearing wind might not impede her. It was dangerous work for the next mile. Every yard of the way she had to splash through the foam, because the great waves were rolling up very nearly to the foot of the cliffs. An extra strong sea might have caught her off her feet, but she did not think of that; she only thought of saving her breath by escaping the direct onslaught of the wind. When she came to the mouth of the burn her heart failed her for a little. There was three-quarters of a mile of water covered with creamy foam, and she did not know but what she might be taken out of her depth. Yet she determined to risk it, and plunged in at a run. The sand was hard under foot, but, as she said, when the piled foam came softly up to her waist she "felt gey funny." Half-way across she stumbled into a hole caused by a swirling eddy, and she thought all was over; but her nerve never failed her, and she struggled till she got a footing again. When she reached the hard ground she was wet to the neck, and her hair was sodden with her one plunge "overhead." Her clothes troubled her with their weight in crossing the moor; so she put off all she did not need and pressed forward again. Presently she reached the house where the coxswain of the lifeboat lived. She gasped out, "The schooner! On the Letch! Norrad."

The coxswain, who had seen the schooner go past, knew what was the matter. He said, "Here, wife, look after the lass," and ran out. The "lass" needed looking after, for she had fainted. But her work was well done; the lifeboat went round the point, ran north, and took six men ashore from the schooner. The captain had been washed overboard, but the others were saved by Dorothy's daring and endurance.

THE SILENT MEN.

TWO very reckless fellows used always to go
fishing together, and used also to spend their
leisure together. One was known as Roughit; and
the other was called Lance. Roughit was big, with
heavy limbs and a rather brutal face. He wore his
hair and beard very long, and his eyes looked
morosely from under thick reddish eyebrows. He
scarcely ever spoke to anybody; and some of the
superstitious fishermen did not like to meet him in the
morning, because they thought he always brought
them bad luck. Lance was a handsome man, with small
hands and feet. He was not like the shaggy giants
of the village—and, indeed, it had been said that
some people at the Hall knew more about his parentage
than might at first sight be supposed. The two men
never talked much, and never exchanged any kind of
greeting when they met and parted. Both of them
were such expert boatmen that excepting on very dark
nights they scarcely needed to communicate except
by signs.

On summer afternoons when the herrings were
coming southward Roughit would knock at Lance's
door and pass on without a word. Presently Lance
would come out, with his oilskins over one arm and his

water-bottle swung by his side.   The coble was lifted
on to the launching-wheels and run down to the water;
then the two men took their places, and the boat stole
away northward over the bay.   They never carried
their fish to any big port, because their boat was so
small that it was not worth their while.   They always
ran back to their own village and sold their catch to
the farmers and labourers in their own neighbourhood.
When the boat was beached, Roughit and Lance had
their nets driven up to the great green and then
spread in the sun for an hour or two.   They sat
smoking and listening to the larks that sung against
one another over the common.   About one o'clock
they strode home together and went to bed until it
was time to go north once more.

The herring season is the pleasantest for fishermen.
It is their harvest; and they have little real hardship
and a good deal of excitement.   On calm nights, after
the nets are shot, there are hours of keen expectancy,
until the oily flicker on the surface of the water tells
that the great shoal is moving to its fate; then
there is the wild bustle among the whole fleet while
the nets are hauled in ; and then comes the pleasant
morning lounge after the fish are sold.

Roughit and Lance were always lucky, and made
lots of money during the summer and autumn.   In
winter times were harder for them.   They mostly did
all their work in the daytime, and sent their fish round
to their customers in the afternoons.   In the evenings
they sat on the bench in the tavern and smoked
silently until the time came for expeditions of another
sort.   The friends were great poachers, and they

carried on their operations like a pair of vicious and well-trained lurchers. Roughit had a small lightly built dog, bred between a collie and greyhound; Lance had a big Bedlington terrier; and these two dogs were certain to be the death of any hare they made up their minds to catch. Lance and Roughit would sit down by the fence beside a gate; the lurcher lay quietly down beside the gate-post, while the terrier slipped through the gap in the hedge and sneaked quietly round to the top of the field. When he had reached the furthermost hedge, he began to beat slowly down towards his confederate : there would come a quick thud, thud of feet; then a scraping on the bars of the gate; then a shrill squeak; and the lurcher cantered quietly up with his game to the place where the two fishermen sat. If old Sam, the Squire's game-keeper, had ever had a chance of putting a charge of shot into either of the dogs he would not have thrown it away. But the brutes usually stayed indoors all day, and never went rummaging the coverts on their own account. Roughit showed no signs of sporting in-stinct; but Lance really liked the fun, and was willing to run all kinds of risks.

Year after year the friends lived their silent life, dividing their time between fishing, poaching, and drinking. Sometimes a spell of bad weather came, and all day long the spray flew over the cottages and the cold breeze covered the sand with foam. The waters roared drearily, and the nights were bad enough to prevent the most inveterate poacher from turning out. During the daytime Lance and Roughit would lounge on the rock-tops, and look grimly out at the

horizon, where the grey clouds laid their shoulders to
the sea.   Their companionship was much like that of
lower animals : it was quite sufficient for one to know
that the other was near.   They did once separate for
a short time.   Roughit shipped in a merchant brig
that was going round to Plymouth.   The vessel made
the run in about a week; but Roughit felt very
wretched during the whole time, without knowing
exactly why.   At Plymouth he deserted, leaving his
box behind him, and set off on foot northwards.

One evening Lance was sitting sulkily on the ground,
when he saw a man crossing the moor.   A vague
curiosity caused him to walk out to meet the stranger,
and presently Roughit came up looking very dirty, and
wearing only an old sleeved waistcoat and a ragged
pair of canvas trousers.   He was barefooted too, and
limped a good deal.   The two men simply nodded and
turned back to the village together.   Neither of them
asked any questions, but they sat drinking until a late
hour, and went home less steadily than might have
been wished.   The people in the Row took but little
notice of this eccentric couple; for, after all, the
friends did harm to nothing except the Squire's
ground-game.

When the two men were growing grizzled with
advancing years the coble which belonged to them had
gone away from the fishing-ground one black night,
before a strong north-easterly gale : she shot between
the Great Farne Island and the Bird's Rock.   The
tide was going like a mill-race, and the solemn roar of
the vast stream made very terrible music in the dark.
The men might have got into their own haven by an

easy passage, despite the gale. But both of them seemed to be always possessed by a gloomy kind of recklessness, and when they made the village lights they determined upon trying an entrance which was desperately difficult. In the centre of a gap which was twenty feet wide stood a rock which was known as "The Tailor's Needle." It stood 400 yards south of "The Cobbler." This rock was clad in sea-weed around its base; but eight feet of the upper part of it was bare of weeds and covered only with tiny shells which tore the hands. On the top of the rock was a very small platform of about one foot square, and in fine weather daring boys would stand upright on this summit and wave to the people ashore. The rock was covered two feet by an ordinary spring tide; but on the night when Roughit and Lance decided to try and pass it, about a foot was above water. There was not a great deal of sea on; indeed, there was hardly more than what the fishermen call a "northerly lipper;" but the tide was running with extraordinary swiftness. Roughit put the helm down and guessed at his bearings. The boat lay hard down and tore in through the gap. There was a long grinding crash; the weather-side lifted clean out of the water; she dropped off the rock, and the two men were pitched overboard. Roughit scrambled to the top, at the expense of torn hands. He hung on as well as he could; but the spray from the combings of the seas cut his face and blinded him. Still, he could easily have held on till dawn, because the tide had no further to rise. Lance, like too many of the fishermen, could not swim. He got hold of the edge of the rock. There was not room for him on the ledge; so presently he said, " I am going." Roughit answered: " No, don't do that; let me give you a haul up here." As Lance went up on one side Roughit went off on the other. The waves buffeted him away towards the shore, and he cried out " Good-night!" when he had swum a few yards westward.

At dawn Lance was picked off " The Tailor's Needle," but Roughit was found dead on the sand. Lance never forgave himself for having taken his comrade's offer; he disliked the village, he hated the sea; and before long he went away inland to work down in the pits.

THE CABIN-BOY.

THE master of a smack was lately accused of having murdered an apprentice; so the mob made desperate attempts to lynch the prisoner every time he was brought before the magistrates. They heard that the dead boy used to be beaten with ropes'-ends, kicked, dragged along the deck, drenched with cold water, and subjected to other ingenious modes of discipline, and they were horrified. Yet only a few years ago no surprise or indignation greeted a skipper who habitually ill-used his cabin-boys. If screams were heard coming from a collier in the Pool, the men in neighbouring vessels scarcely took the trouble to turn round. They knew that some unhappy boy was being corrected; and they believed in stripes and bruises as necessary agencies in nautical education. When a weakly lad chanced to die he was dropped overboard, and there was an end of the matter; the strong lads who lived through these brutalities grew into fine sailors.

Times are altered. The old-fashioned sailor is an extinct creature, and modern conditions have developed a totally new variety. The old-fashioned sailor was brought up in an atmosphere of rough cruelty; the new-fashioned sailor will submit to no tyranny what-

ever. The old-fashioned skipper was very like the
Hull culprit in habits and customs; the new-fashioned
skipper is overbearing and often conceited, but rarely
brutal.

They formed a strange society, did those East
Coast sailors of past days. A boy grew up in one of
the brisk little ports that lay between Wivenhoe and
Spittal. The notion of inland life had no place in his
mind, for his thoughts in early years suffered a sea
change. He played on the quay, and heard the
growling talk of the lounging, bearded sailors; so
that he soon became critical in the matter of ships and
seamanship. He could tell you the name of every black
and apple-bowed vessel that came curtseying over the
bar on the flood tide; and he would prove the
superiority of the "Halicore" over the "Mary Jane,"
with many clenching allusions to aged authorities. If
the black fleet went out with a northerly breeze blowing, he could name the ship that would be first clear
of the ruck; if the wind were off the land, he knew
which ship would be suited by having the breeze on
the beam. Long before he ever saw the outside of
the bar he had heard of every point on the coast. The
possibility of becoming anything but a sailor never
entered his head. He tried to copy the flat-footed
rolling walk of the seamen, and he longed for the time
when he might wear a braided cap and smoke a pipe.
While yet little more than a child he went on his trial
voyage, and had his first experience of sea-sickness.
Then he was bound apprentice for five years, his wages
beginning at £8 per year, and increasing yearly by £2
until the end of his term. His troubles began after

his indentures were signed. The average skipper had
no thought of cruelty and yet was very cruel. The
poor lad had a very scanty allowance of water for
washing; yet if he appeared at breakfast-time with
face and hands unclean he was sent squeaking up to
the galley with a few smart weals tingling upon him.
All sorts of projectiles were launched at him merely to
emphasize orders. The mate, the able seamen (or
" full-marrows "), the ordinary seamen (or " half-
marrows ") never dreamed of signifying their pleasure
to him save with a kick or an open-handed blow. His
only time of peace came when it was his watch below,
and he could lay his poor little unkempt head easily in
his hammock. In bad weather he took his chance
with the men. The icy gusts roared through the
rigging; the cold spray smote him and froze on him;
green seas came over and forced him to hold on where-
soever he might. Sometimes the clumsy old brig
would drown everybody out of the forecastle, and the
little sailor had to curl up in his oilskins on the
streaming floor of the after-cabin. Sometimes the ship
would have to " turn " every yard of the way from
Thames to Tyne, or from Thames to Blyth. Then
the cabin-boy had to stamp and shiver with the rest
until the vessel came round on each new tack, and
then perhaps he would be forced to haul on a rope
where the ice was, hardening. It might be that on
one bad night, when the fog lay low on the water and
the rollers lunged heavily shoreward, the skipper
would make a mistake. The look-out men would hear
the thunder of broken water close under the bows;
and then, after a brief agony of hurry and effort, the

vessel beat herself to bits on the remorseless stones.
In that case the little cabin-boy's troubles were soon
over.   The country people found him in the morning
stretched on the beach with his eyes sealed with the
soft sand.   But in most instances he made his trips
from port to port safely enough.   His chief danger
came when he lay in the London river or in the Tyne.
As soon as a collier was moored in the Pool or in the
Blackwall Reach, the skipper made it a point of honour
to go ashore, and the boy had to scull the ship's boat
to the landing.   From the top of Greenwich Pier to
the bend of the river a fleet of tiny boats might be
seen bobbing at their painters every evening.   The
skippers were ashore in the red-curtained public-
houses.   The roar of personal experiences sounded
through the cloud of tobacco-smoke and steam, and
the drinking was steady and determined.   Out on the
river the shadows fell on the racing tide; the weird
lights flickered in the brown depths of the water; and
the swirling eddies gurgled darkly and flung the boats
hither and thither.   In the stern of each boat was
a crouching figure; for the little cabin-boy had to
wait in the cold until the pleasures of rum and conversation had palled upon his master.   Sometimes the
boy fell asleep; there came a lurch, he fell into the
swift tide, and was borne away into the dark.   Over
and over again did little boys lose their lives in this
way when their thoughtless masters kept them waiting
until midnight or later.

Through hunger and cruelty and storm and stress,
the luckier cabin-boy grew in health and courage until
his time was out.   When he went home he wore a

thick blue coat, wide blue trousers, and a flat cap with
mystic braid ; and on the quay he strolled with his
peers in great majesty. Tiny children admired his
earrings and his cap and his complicated swagger.
Then in due time came the blessed day when he called
himself ordinary seaman, and when the most energetic
of mates dared not thrash him (unless, indeed, the
mate happened to be much the stronger man, in which
case professional etiquette was apt to be disregarded) ;
his pay rose to £2 a month ; he felt justified in walking
regularly with a maiden of his choice ; and his brown
face showed signs of moustache and beard. Then he
became A.B., then mate, and last of all he reached the
glories of mastership and £8 a month. By that time
he had become a resolute, skilful man, with coarse
tastes and blunt feelings. Danger never cost him
a thought. He would swear fearfully about trifling
annoyances ; but in utmost peril, when his ship was
rolling yard-arm under, or straining off the gnashing
cliffs of a lee-shore, he was quiet and cool and resigned.
He took the risk of his life as part of his day's work
and made no fuss about it. He was hopelessly ignorant
and wildly conservative ; he believed in England, and
reckoned foreigners as a minor species. His sinful
insularity ran to ludicrous manifestations sometimes.
An old coaster was once beating up for his own
harbour and trying to save the tide. A little Danish
brig got a slant of wind and rattled in over the bar,
while the collier had to stand off for six hours. The
captain was gravely indignant at this mischance, and,
sighing, said, " Ah ! God cares far more for them
furriners than He does for His own countrymen."

As he grew in years his temper became worse, and his girth greater. The violent exertion of his earlier days was exchanged for the ease of a man who had nothing to do but stand about, eat, sleep, and throw things at cabin-boys. He had all the peremptory disposition of an Eastern tyrant; and the notion of being called to account for any one of his doings would have thrown him into apoplectic surprise. So he lived out his days, working his old tub up and down the coast with marvellous skill, beating his boy, roaring songs when his vessel lay in the Pool, and lamenting the good times gone by. When at last his joints grew too stiff, and other troubles of age came upon him, he settled ashore in some little cottage and devoted himself to quiet meditation of a pessimistic kind. Every morning he rolled down to the quay and criticised with cruel acuteness the habits of the younger generation of mariners; every evening he took his place in the tavern parlour and instructed the assembled skippers. At last the time came for him to go : then the men whom he had scored with ropes'-ends in his day were the first to mourn him and to speak with admiration of his educational methods.

The skipper of the new school is a sad backslider. He would think it undignified to beat a boy; he wears a black frock coat, keeps novels in his cabin, wears a finger-ring, and tries to look like a ship-broker. He mixes his north-country accent with a twang learned in the West-end theatres, and he never goes ashore without a tall hat and an umbrella. His walk is a grievous trouble to his mind. The ideal ship-broker has a straight and seemly gait; but no captain who ever tried to imitate the ship-broker could quite do away with a certain nautical roll. The new-fashioned captain is not content with that simple old political creed of true sailors, which began and ended with the assertion that one Englishman could beat any six foreigners. This is crude in his eyes. He knows all about Gladstone and the Land Bill; he is abreast of his age in knowledge of the Eastern Question ; and he claims kindred with a Party. His self-confidence is phenomenal, but not often offensive. In short, he is a sort of nautical bagman, with all the faults and all the businesslike virtues of his kind.

THE SQUIRE.

EVERY afternoon when the weather was bright, an erect old man used to ride round the Fisher Row on a stout cob. If the men happened to be sitting in the sun, on the benches, he would stop and speak to them, in sharp, ringing accents, and he always had a word for the women as they sat baiting their lines in the open air. He called the men by their Christian names, and they called him by the name of his estate. None of the fishermen ever ventured to be familiar with him; but he often held long talks with them about commonplace matters. They considered that they had a proprietary interest in him, and they always inquired about his family affairs. He would tell them that Mr. Harry had gone with his regiment to India, or that Miss Mabel had gone to stay with her aunt at the West Moor, or, that Miss Ella was coming home from school for altogether next month. All this cross-questioning was carried on without the least vulgarity. The people were really anxious to hear news of the boys and girls who had grown up amongst them, and they thought it would please the Squire if they treated him as a sort of Patriarch.

The old man lived for nearly a century in the one place. It may be said that not long before he died he wagered that he would reach his hundredth year, but he missed that by three years. His whole energy and thought were devoted to improving his estate. He had no notion of art or things of that kind, yet he managed to make his village and its surroundings very beautiful by long years of care. The sleepy place where he lived was right away from the currents of modern life. If you walked over a mile of moorland, then through five miles of deep wood, where splendid elms and fine beeches made shade for you, you would come at last to some rising ground, and, if you waited, you might see far away the trailing smoke of a train. But there are men now, on the Squire's estate, who have never seen an engine, and there must be a score or so of the population who have never slept one night away from their native place. While Mr. Pitt was breaking his heart over Austerlitz; while Napoleon was playing his last throw at Waterloo; while the Birmingham men were threatening to march on London, the Squire was riding peacefully day by day, in the lanes and spinneys of his lovely countryside. He never would allow a stranger to settle on his property, and he was never quite pleased if any of the fisher girls married pitmen. He did not mind when the hinds and the fishers intermarried, but anything that suggested noise and smoke was an abhorrence to him, and thus he disliked the miners. A splendid seam of coal ran beneath his land. This coal could have been easily won; in fact, at the place where the cliffs met the sea, a two-foot seam cropped out, and the people could go with a pickaxe and break off a basketful for themselves whenever they chose; but the Squire would never allow borings to be made. He did not object to the use of coal on abstract grounds, but he was determined that his property should not be disfigured. Once, when a smart agent came to make proposals respecting the sinking of a pit, the Squire took him by the shoulders and solemnly pushed him out of his study. He fancied that a colliery would bring poachers and squalor and drunkenness, and many other bad consequences, so he kept his fields unsullied and his little streams pure. Without knowing it, the Squire was a bit of a poet. For example, he had one long dell, which ran through his woods, planted with hyacinths and the wild pink geranium. These flowers came in bloom together, and the effect of the great sheet of blue and pink was indescribable. He was very proud of this piece of work, and he always looked happy as he went down the path in the spring time.

The Squire had the most intimate acquaintance with the circumstances of every man, woman, and child on his property. If he rode out at two in the afternoon and heard that a fisherman was suffering with rheumatism, it was almost certain that the fat manservant from the Hall would call at the sick man's house before the day was out with blankets and wine, and whatever else might be needed. Yet the Squire was by no means lavish. In making a bargain with a tenant he never showed the least generosity. On one occasion he set a number of gardeners to work in a very large orchard where the trees were beginning to feel the effects of time. The men were likely to be employed for at least three years, so each of them was fixed by a formal engagement. The married men were paid fifteen shillings a week, but on coming to a young man, the Squire said, "Now I am going to give you a shilling a week less than the others because you live with your mother." This sounds like the speech of a very stingy person; but in spite of the apparent hardness of the great landlord, poverty was never known on his estate. The hinds had to eat barley bread, and beef and mutton were not plentiful, for the butcher's visit only came once in the week. Yet nevertheless the men were healthy and powerful, and the women and children were neatly and decently dressed.

Once every year the Squire met the whole of his tenants. As Michaelmas came round he drew his rents, and then the dandy agent, the solid farmers, and the poor cottiers sat down at one table for the rent dinner. The strict discipline of ordinary life was relaxed, and the Squire allowed even the fishermen to make jokes in his presence. When the company broke up in the evening it often happened that various members were obliged to lie down in the hedge-sides, and once the Squire had to ride his cob right over his own head mason. The mason happened to be thinking about nautical affairs when the grey cob swept down upon him, and just as the Squire cleared him he cried "Ship ahoy." This occurrence supplied the Squire with a joke which lasted nearly forty years.

All the sayings which the Squire dropped at the rent dinner were carefully treasured, and formed the subject of occasional conversation on the benches until the year went round again.

The good man did not like newspapers. When he

began his life as a landlord at the end of the last
century, the folk who lived on the estate managed
perfectly well without journals, and he did not see why
a change should be made. He never could understand
why a man could not be content with his own life, and
his own sensations, instead of wanting to know what
other people in other parts of the world were saying
and doing.

About the time of the Reform agitation of 1867 he
rode round to the masons' shed. The men were
having their eleven o'clock meal, and as they ate their
bread and cheese, Fat Jack, the stone-cutter, read to
them one of Mr. John Bright's speeches. The Squire
did not exactly know, or care to know, who Mr. John
Bright might be, but he gathered enough from Fat
Jack's guttural elocution to cause uneasiness. He
declared that if ever the postman brought such a thing
into the village again he would never allow a letter to
be delivered on his estate. But with all this bluster,
the common people knew that their landlord wished
them well, and they were ready to do anything for
him.

One night, while he was dragging his trout stream,
he fell into the ugliest part of the water. He had
hardly had time to come to the surface when six men
were in after him, and he had to thank each one of the
six in the same formal terms before any of them would
consent to resign the whole credit of the rescue.

His eldest son was killed in battle. Before departing
for the fatal campaign, the young officer had dragged
the burn, and placed all the brown trout that he caught
in a great tarn that lay amongst the low hills on the

moor. The fish increased and multiplied until the little lake was swarming. Big fat trout used to roll easily round on summer evenings, and make lazy lunges at the flies. It would have been easy to have taken twenty dozen out of the lake in a day; but the Squire said he did not want the pond fished because his boy had stocked it. So no native ever cast a line there, although the temptation was almost unbearable.

A very smart young person came from the neighbouring market town once, and tried the pond with the fly. He had just reached his third dozen when he was caught by old Sam, the gamekeeper, and three fishermen. They tied a cart-rope round his waist and threw him into the pond; they then pitched the whole of the trout back into the water, and after that they dragged the trespasser out, floured him carefully, and sent him on his road.

These incidents are not idyllic, but they serve to show what kind of a hold a strong, just man may obtain upon simple people if he only shows that he is ready to work for them. The whole of the tenantry and the villagers knew that their stern old master gave up his life for their sake. They knew that he worked like a common bailiff; they knew that he drank nothing but water; they knew that he put by money every year with the sole object of making improvements which might better their condition, and they respected him accordingly.

When he reached the age of ninety-six years he was no longer capable of guiding his pony: the pony guided him. On one afternoon the beast turned just at the end of the Fisher Row and walked the old man quietly back to the stables. He could not dismount without assistance, and he had to wait in the stall, while Matchem munched his oats, until one of the stable boys came and released him. From that day the Squire rode no more, and the occasion was memorable, alike for fishers and hinds.

When the old man died he was followed to his grave by the entire population from nine farms and two fishing villages. Old men of eighty, who remembered him when he was a bright young fellow in George the Third's time, went and stood round his grave. Everybody wanted some remembrance of him, but this could not be attained until the clever national schoolmaster of the village suggested that an engraving should be made from a photograph. You cannot go into one cottage or one farm-house on the whole of the estate without finding an engraved portrait of the splendid old man hung in a place of honour.

THE VILLAGE PREACHER.

THE Methodists got a very strong hold in sea-side places at the end of the last century, but during the long pressure of the great War the claims of religion were somewhat forgotten. Smuggling went on to an extraordinary extent, and the consequent demoralisation was very apparent. The strict morality which the stern Methodists of the old school taught had been broken, and some of the villages were little better than nests of pirates. The decent people who lived inland were continually molested by marauding ruffians who came from sea-side places, and to call a man a "fisher," was to label him with a term of reproach.

On Saturday nights every Fisher Row was a scene of drunken turmoil, and on Sunday the men lounged about drinking, the women scolding, while the old-fashioned simplicity of life seemed to be forgotten altogether.

Grave countrymen shook their heads over the terrible change. Our village had become notorious for bad behaviour, and the old man who tried to keep up the traditions of religion was much distressed in his mind.

This local preacher was coming over the moor one

fine summer night when the moon shone so as to make the sands and the trees round the village look splendid. The peacefulness of the night seemed to have impressed him, and he was occupied with his own grave thoughts.

As he passed the tavern the front door opened, and a waft of rank tobacco came out. Then came a little mob of fishermen, many of whom were cursing and swearing. Two of them began to fight, and the local preacher heard the thud of heavy blows. He stepped in amongst the crowd and tried to separate the fighters, but he only got jeered at for his pains. He was usually very civilly treated, but the men were in drink and could not discriminate.

The next day was Sunday, and as the evening dropped down there was a stir in the village, and a score or two of the villagers came out on the green. Three or four men took to playing pitch and toss, and the women got up little quarrels on their own account. A few big fellows walked towards the shore, and got ready the boats to go out fishing, for there was no respect shown to the Sabbath.

At seven o'clock the local preacher took his stand in the middle of the green, and remained there bareheaded until he had attracted attention. He began to pray aloud, and the villagers stood grinning round him until he had finished. He then asked the people to join him in a hymn, but this proposal was too comic, and the men and women laughed loudly.

The preacher, however, was not a man to be stopped by a little laughter. He actually did sing a hymn in a beautiful tenor, and, before he had finished, some of the men seemed rather ashamed of having laughed at all.

One of the leaders said—" Let us hear what this born fool has to say. If he makes very much noise we'll take and put him in one of the rain-water barrels." A poacher proposed that the dogs should be set on him; but, although this idea was received as a humorous contribution to the discussion, it was not put into practice.

· The preacher began a kind of rude address. He picked his words with a certain precision, and managed to express himself in the dialect of the people to whom he was speaking. His enthusiasm grew, and at the end of a quarter of an hour he had obtained such complete mastery over the crowd, that individuals amongst the audience unconsciously imitated the changes of his face.

The man was really a kind of poet, and the villagers felt his power without exactly knowing why. When the preaching was over, the orator strode away home without speaking to anybody.

On the next Sunday he appeared in the same place at the same hour. Only some half a dozen men and lads were on the green, and these were gambling as usual; but when they saw the preacher, two or three of them ran along the Row and brought out the people. The men who had intended to go fishing stayed out of curiosity; and not a single boat was run off the sands that night. The next week the best part of the village population was waiting when the preacher came. Some of the very old men were accommodated with logs of wood which had been

E

brought out for seats, and the very roughest of the young men remained respectfully silent.

Some heavy clouds came over the hills and discharged a sprinkle of water upon the group.   A big man stepped out and spoke to the preacher.   He was one of the most powerful fellows on the coast, and had been a great ruffian in his time.   It was said that he once killed a man with a single blow.   He offered the preacher the use of his house, and presently all the villagers were packed in the great sanded kitchen, and a rude service was carried on under cover.

The work thus begun went on for years.   Sometimes a little spasmodic emotion was shown in the meetings by women who were hysterically inclined, but in general the services were free from excitement and vulgarity.   The little tavern had to be shut up, for the men stopped drinking.

The fishermen saw the preacher roughly dressed during the week and doing work as hard as their own, yet the influence he gained over them was so strong that it came to be regarded as a very discreditable thing for any man or woman to stay away from the evening services.

By-and-by the fisherman who had been the worst ruffian in the village used to take a turn at the preaching.   His remarks would have been very laughable to outsiders, but as he was a man of strong character and genuine feeling, his hearers took him quite seriously.

As the preacher grew old he was regarded with extreme reverence, especially by the women, whose lives had often been very hard before the Revival.

One night the big man, who had first offered the preacher shelter, was sitting in the kitchen when a neighbour came in. The new-comer seemed flurried, and said—" I am going to hit you very hard. The old man's dying. He says he wants to see you ; so come you away with me." The giant didn't put his hat on, and did not even take off his sea-boots. He ran out at once, and strode heavily over the moor. The old man was waiting for him, but the end was very near.

The preacher made a pathetic little joke. He said, " You once gave me shelter. Maybe I'll have to get one of the many mansions ready for you." Soon after that the ebb tide began to run out, and the preacher died in the big fisherman's arms.

When the day of the funeral came, the men would not allow the corpse to be put in the hearse ; they took turns to carry the coffin over the moor, and the women and children followed in lines.

There was a little jealousy as to who should have the old man's dog, but there was very little need for that, because the collie went from house to house in the Row, arranging his visits with a view to meal-times.

After a while a good Church of England clergyman took up the work that the Primitive had begun. The fishers did not like the university man, with his dainty accent, quite so well as their rough friend, but they always behaved well to him, and they are still a very decent and sober set of people.

THE FISHER'S FRIEND.

A SQUARE stone house decked with clambering honeysuckle stood in a lonely place about a mile to the northward of the Row. A narrow flower garden lay to the right and left of the front, and in spring-time and summer a delicate little lady used to come out and move gracefully about among the flower beds. She was old, but she carried herself erect, and her cheeks were prettily tinged. Her dress was in the style of the last century, and she made no change in her fashions from year's end to year's end. On Sundays she walked primly to church, wearing a quaint deep bonnet from which her pretty face peeped archly. She reminded you of some demure chapter in an old-world book. After she had finished with her flowers in the mornings she would walk through the kitchen garden and thence into her orchard. Four or five tortoise-shell cats and two sleek spaniels followed her around, and took a dignified interest in her proceedings. When the lady had visited the cows in the paddock she walked through the dairy and got ready to go out. When she came out she bore a little basket on her arm, and she went to visit her old women, and her favourite children. Whenever she stepped into Black Mary's kitchen that aged dame was sure to be smoking, and the little lady would say, "Now Mary, you'll shorten your life if you keep on with that bad habit." Mary would answer, "Well, well, I'm a long way over seventy now, a day or two won't make a great deal of difference." This joke pleased both parties very much, and it was always followed by the production of enough tobacco to last Mary for a day—unless the fisher lads chanced to steal some. After that the cottager's children had to be seen, and those young persons looked at the basket with interest. The dainty visitor would say, "Now Jimmy, I saw you pelting the ducks this morning. How would you like some big cruel man to pelt you? And I saw you, Frank, wading without ever doubling your trousers up; you will catch cold, and your mother and I will have to give you nasty medicine." After this stern reproof some little packets were brought out of the basket and shared with care.

Thus the old lady went about the place like a sort of fairy godmother. The fishermen were fond of her. Big Tom, the giant, used to look kindly down at her from under his great brows, and listened to her sharp, twittering speech as though he were criticising some new species of bird. All the other fishermen treated her with rough politeness, and they called her Miss Anne, without troubling themselves about her second name. She was known to the tramps who travelled the coast road, and the gipsies made much of her in their sly, Eastern way. Whenever a poor man knocked she called off the dogs, and went out to talk with him; she questioned him briskly; asked about his parents, his birthplace, his age, the distance he had travelled,

his destination, and all sorts of other matters. She
then took him to the great wooden table outside the
dairy if she was satisfied, and gave him food and a
little money. Sometimes she heard that her guests
spent the money in the village tavern, but she did not
alter her charitable habits for all that. She would say,
" Oh sad, sad man, to spend his money like that."
Then she would add, " But, perhaps he hasn't learned
any other pleasure."

The gipsies used to send for medicine when any of
them were ailing, and they repaid her kindness by
leaving her live stock alone. Once she lost some of
her silver-pencilled chickens, but they were soon
returned, and it was said that the man who stole them
had a very bad beating from one of the Lees who had
been a prizefighter. A few marks on the lintel of the
door let all the regular tramps know that Miss Anne's
property must not be touched; and she very rarely
locked her doors in winter. The dark nights were
weary for young folks, so Miss Anne used often to
invite some favourites among the village boys to come
and spend an hour or two in her delightful parlour.
The wind screamed hoarsely among the elder-bushes,
and the wintry sea made strange noises on the sands,
but the happy boys in the bright room never much
heeded the weather outside. When Miss Anne had
made sure that her guests had spotless hands she let
them visit her book-shelves, and they could look
through the precious volumes of Bewick's Natural
History. A great number of stuffed specimens orna-
mented the walls of the room, and nothing pleased
Miss Anne better than to show how the stuffed birds

resembled the woodcuts of the wonderful engraver.
After a little time the mistress would question the lads
about the various animals. She would say, " Now,
Ralph, you shall tell me all about the old English
mastiff, and if you break down I shall have to ask
Jimmy;" but when the invariable distribution of
tarts came, no difference was made between the boys
who failed and those who did not. At nine o'clock
the young people lit their lanterns and went off over
the dark moor.

Thus Miss Anne lived her life from week to week in
that remote place. Her only excitement came when
very bad weather broke on us. If vessels were in
danger off our savage rocks, she would stand on the
cliffs while the spray lashed up in her face and drenched
her with its bitter saltness. If a shipwrecked crew
were brought ashore she always liked to take in one
or two of the men, and her house was kept in a sad
turmoil until her guests had gone away. There are
Italians, Norwegians, Swedes, and Frenchmen, besides
our own countrymen, who remember the exquisite
lady with gratitude. Very few people knew how Miss
Anne came to live unmarried, and in solitude; but
there is a sorrowful story that explains all. The
Fisher's Friend had been the greatest beauty in all the
north country, and many men had loved her. One mad
young fellow asked her to marry him. She liked him,
but she had always said that she never would have him
for a husband unless he gave up his wild ways. Again
and again they quarrelled, and made friends when he
promised to be better. At last she said something
very bitter to him, and ordered him out of her sight.

He tramped in his own woods all night, and in the morning he galloped his big brown horse down to the sea. He met Miss Anne and straightened his horse across her path. She spoke sharply to him again, so he dashed the spurs in, and went away. Next morning Miss Anne heard that he had hung himself in the barn, and that he had left a note upbraiding her. She turned very white, and went to her room, where she stayed praying all day. The young Squire's death really ended her life.

After she had grown old, she failed one morning to rise early, and the servants, who had been used to hear the quick sound of her feet whenever the dawn came, grew alarmed. They sent for Big Tom, and Tom broke open Miss Anne's bedroom door about noon. She was lying dead, and on her breast they found a miniature portrait of a handsome and dark-looking young man. She had worn her sweetheart's likeness for fifty years.

THE COASTGUARD.

WINTER and summer, every night about six o'clock, a tall man, dressed in blue, strode over the moor. Sometimes he looked on the ground for a long time together, and seemed to be buried in deep thought. When he came to the stream he always found another man waiting for him on the far side, and this man was accompanied by a rough water-spaniel. The two friends, who were both coastguards, held a little chat, and then the dog was told to go over for the letters. The spaniel swam across, received the blue despatches, and carried them to his master; then, with a cheery good-night, the men turned back and went across the dark moor to their homes.

In the morning the tall coastguard was astir very early. He walked along the rock tops with his old telescope under his arm, and looked acutely at the vessels that crept round the bay. During the middle of the day he had little to do. In fine weather he would sit outside his door with a book, and in bad weather he was always to be found, from ten to four o'clock, on the long settle beside the great fire in his little cottage. He was one of the old school, and had entered the service at the time when civilians

were admitted, so he had the utmost contempt for the
new school of boatmen who came from on board men-
of-war. He was rarely troubled with visits from
inspecting officers; in fact, after a certain memorable
occurrence, the commander of the station let him
alone. A very shrewd officer wished to show his own
cleverness, and to find out his men's weakness; so
one night, when thick clouds were flying across the
moon, he crept round the bay in a six-oared cutter,
ran ashore on the sand, hauled up half a dozen empty
kegs, and told his men to bury them in the sand.
This ingenious captain proceeded as he fancied smugglers would have done, and he intended to go round
to the coastguard's cottage and inform him of the
trick in the morning. Just as the casks had been
triumphantly covered, a voice called sharply, " Who
goes there ?"

The clever officer was thrown off his guard, and
was too confused to speak.

The challenge was repeated, and presently a couple
of bullets whizzed sharply among the party. The
coastguard had emptied both his pistols, and one of
the bullets cut through the officer's shoulder-knot.

The modern coastguardmen never expect to find
such an animal as a smuggler : all contraband business
is done by dint of craft and not by daring. Firemen
and engineers scoop out coal from the bottom of a
ship's bunkers and fill the space up with tobacco.
Sometimes a clever carpenter will actually hollow out
a beam in the forecastle or a block of wood which is
used as a stool; the whole article looks perfectly solid,
and the Custom-house officers are apt to pass it by.

But our friend the coastguard had been used to the old-fashioned smugglers—desperate men who would let fly a ball on the very slightest provocation.

Before the piping times of peace came he had known what it was to charge with a party right amongst a gang of desperate fellows who were bumping kegs ashore.

When in the grey of the evening the low black lugger crept stealthily towards the shore, the coastguard had been used to stalk the gliding vessel like some wild beast. He could not row off and board her, because the lugger would have spread her brown wings and flown away into the uttermost dark. The coastguardsmen had to catch the smugglers in the act of bringing their goods ashore, and in order to do this he had to contend against a conspiracy of the villagers, who were always ready to lend their horses and their labour to those who were cheating the king. No amount of logic could ever persuade the small farmer that smuggling was in any way immoral, so the coastguard had to combat the cunning of the bold sailors who ran across from Cherbourg, and the still greater cunning of the slouching fellows who signalled his movements from the shore. This was his training, and when the time came for smuggling to be given over entirely to merchant seamen instead of being carried on by desperadoes, the change left the old officer still ready and resolute, and quick with his pistol.

It was well for the Revenue that one at least of their servants retained the habits and instincts of the ancient race of preventive-men.

One night, just as the tide was flowing, our friend stepped out of his cottage and looked across the bay. Suddenly he saw a light, which flashed for a short time and then was darkened; another flash came and then another; the flood was pouring south in a sombre stream; there was not a gleam on the water, and the whole sea looked like a huge dark abyss. From the depths of the troubled blackness the coastguard saw another light flash back in answer to the one which had been waved from the shore; the seaward light was simply like the ordinary mast-head lantern of a fishing-boat; but the coastguard noticed that it was waved three times, as if in answer to a set signal. He did not quite like the look of things, so he got out a pony from the stables at the Hall and galloped around till he was near the place from which he guessed that the flashes had come. He lay down amongst the long grass and waited in an agony of expectation for something that might help him to solve the puzzle. It turned out that a set of fellows had determined to go back to the old ways, and the flash that the coastguard saw from the sea was shown from an ordinary herring-boat which now lay perilously close to the beach. He saw the black hull wavering like a shadow amid the uncertain gloom and the solemn water. Presently a hand touched him, and a terrible thrill of momentary terror shook his nerves. The man that touched him gave a sharp cry and recoiled; before he could utter another sound the coastguard was upon him, and the muzzle of a great horse-pistol was clapped to his face. The coastguard said: "Tell me where they are going to land?"

The prostrate man hesitated ; whereupon his stern assailant said : " I'll give you until I count three ! "

The frightened lout stammered : " They are coming past this way."

A few long minutes went by, and then the coastguard heard a sound of laboured breathing ; this sound came from a horse which was dragging a large hay-cart through the heavy sand. Two men walked, one on each side of the horse, and a third pushed the cart from behind. The coastguardman had only two shots to spare, and he did not know in the least whether the men opposed to him were armed or not. His decision had to be made swiftly. He was a kind man, fond of dumb animals, and averse to hurting anything in the world ; but he saw that there was only one way of preventing the cargo from being safely carried inland. It went sorely against him to take an innocent life ; but just as the horse passed him, he fired, aiming a little behind the near shoulder. The horse gave a convulsive stagger and fell dead in the shafts. There was then left one man with a pistol against four, who might or might not be armed. Luckily it happened that the smugglers only carried bludgeons. The coastguard saw that he could not hope to catch any of them, so he said quietly : " I have another shot here, and I am quite safe up to thirty paces. If you don't clear away, I'll have one of you ; but I don't say which one it will be."

This practical address had a very good effect ; the men wisely ran away. The coastguard loaded his other pistol and mounted guard on the cart.

In the morning a passing tramp brought him help ;

the cart was conveyed to the station, and it was found that a splendid haul had been attempted. There was a load of silks and brandy, which was worth a great deal of money. This was the very last attempt at old-fashioned smuggling that ever was made on the north-east coast, and there is no doubt that the attempt would have been successful if only raw young sailors had been employed as guards, instead of an old hand who knew every move of the game.

The coastguardman received his promotion soon afterwards, and he continued to express his contempt for man-o'-war's men and smugglers till he arrived at a very old age.

THE SUSPECTED MAN.

A TALL girl used to wander about from village to village down the coast. Strangers did not know what was the matter with her, but all the people who lived round the bay knew that she was out of her mind. Her clothes were not very good, but she kept herself clean, and when she was in the humour she would help the neighbours. She had no relations living, but she never went short of food, for the fishers and the farm people, and even the pitmen, took care to give her shelter and enough to eat. She was mostly bare-headed, but in September, when the cotton-grass grew feathery, she liked to make herself a head-dress out of the grey plumes. When her Sunday hat, as she called it, was on, she was fond of putting the red fronds of the dying bracken into her belt, and with these adornments she looked picturesque.

She was always humming to herself, but she never got beyond one silly old song which is common enough in the north country. As she walked along the links she used to move her hands in a stupid way to the rhythm of her music. The words that she sung are known to the people who live on the border, but nobody has ever completed the lyric to which they belong. The two verses which she sang were :—

" Oh have you seen my bonny lad,
    And ken ye if he's weel, O !
It's owre the land and owre the sea
    He's gyen to moor the keel, O !

" Oh yes, I saw your bonny lad,
    Upon the sea I spied him,
His grave is green, but not wi' grass,
    And you'll never lie beside him."

The tune to which she sang her lines was rather merry than otherwise, and sometimes she would dance to the measure. The boys were kind to her, and she liked to enter a school-yard during play time, because the young people used to share their sweets with her.

Whenever the weather was very stormy she walked about the sands and tore at her hair. If a ship stood into the bay to escape the northerly wind, she was violently excited ; and, when vessels anchored a good mile out, she would scream warnings to the captains.

She had been a very fine girl in her time, and many of the fisher lads would have been glad to have married her. The sailor-men too from the colliers' port used to come after her. But she went mad when she found the lad whom she liked best lying dead on the beach, and so she never married.

The story of her sweetheart's death was one of the ugliest that ever was known on the shores of the bay. He was a smart fellow, who went mate of a brig that ran to Middlesborough for iron-stone. The brig was not much of a beauty, and, when she had to go round, the odds were always about two to one that she would " miss stays."

In coming northward from Middlesborough, one bad winter's day, she missed stays once too often, and when the captain found that she would not come round, he let go one anchor. But the chain was of no more use than a straw rope : it snapped, and the vessel came ashore, broadside on to the rocks. It was about dusk when she struck, and nothing could be done to help the men.

Mad Mary's sweetheart swam ashore, but it seemed that he must have been very much exhausted when he got to the sand, and somebody was waiting for him who had better never have seen him.

A man who stood under the cliffs while the poor struggling swimmer fought southward, had a bad reputation in every village from Spittal to Cullercoates. He was a sulky fellow, and did not make his living by legitimate ways. None of the men cared to associate with him, for he had once violated every instinct of kindness that the fishermen and sailors held dear.

He had found an abandoned vessel to the north of the Dogger Bank, and he boarded her. Finding no one on deck, he determined to sail the vessel into port and get the salvage on her. A retriever dog came floundering along the deck and fawned upon him. Now the man had heard that if any living thing is on board a vessel no salvage-money can be claimed when the ship is picked up, and he believed the story, so he coaxed the dog, patted him until he got the chance of a fair hold, then put his arms round the poor beast, and pitched it overboard.

The story was told everywhere by the other smacks-men, and the children used to cry, " Who drowned the

dog ? " whenever the doer of this wicked act appeared
in the street.   The fellow who drowned the dog was
certainly close by when the brig touched, but beyond
this we know nothing that could prove a crime.   In
the morning, when a troop of fishermen walked along
the beach to see if anything could be picked up, they
found Mary sitting on the sand beside the dead body
of a man.   The dead sailor's head was bruised, and
his waistcoat had been torn open.   A rat-catcher who
had crossed the moor said that he saw the man who
drowned the dog skulking up the hollow from the
place where the corpse lay, but no one brought any
definite accusation, for, after all, the bruise on the
head might have been caused by a blow on a stone.
Still the suspected man had a bad life after this occurrence.   Mary lost her senses completely, but she
recognized him always, and whenever she saw him she
crooked her fingers like the claws of a cat, and showed
her teeth.   Why she did so could only be guessed :
perhaps she had seen more than the rat-catcher, but
she never said anything.

The fellow who had earned this suspicion stayed in
the village until one memorable winter night, when
some youths waylaid him as he came sneaking off the
moor with his lurcher.   They put a lantern under a
sheet and waited till their scouts told them that the
victim was near.   As soon as he had passed the marsh
that borders the waste, the practical jokers pushed up
a pole with the lantern on top, and with the sheet over
the lantern.   The poacher lay down on his face and
shouted for mercy.   He never came into the village
after this, but went to an inland town and lived by his

old mysterious industry. No crime worse than poaching was ever brought home to him, and, as he left the seafaring life, the unpleasant memory of him soon died away. Mad Mary wandered the countryside for a long time : some kind people wanted to put her in an asylum, because they feared she might get drowned as she walked the shore where the unhappy little brig went to pieces. But she was never put under restraint, and her innocent life passed amid kindness and pity.

THE RABBIT-CATCHER.

I HAD the fancy to walk out one winter's morning in a very lonely place. The wind was laden with sleet, and as I walked on the top of the cliffs it struck my right cheek viciously, and then screamed away past through the furze-bushes. The light was coming up slowly over the leaden sea, and the waves seemed cowed by the steady flogging of the sleet. I heard the woods complaining from afar off, and the whistling curlew as he called overhead made me think of messengers of evil. Presently I came to a great range of rounded hills, which were covered by withered bracken. Certain gaps led through these hills to the beach, and along the beach I determined to walk. My terrier concluded that rabbits were vanity. He drooped his ears and tail, and trotted along as if he were reproaching me for my rashness. I was glancing out over the grey trouble of the sea, and watching the forlorn ships cowering along like belated ghosts, when I heard a click to the right of me. Looking up the bluff, I saw a tall powerful lad who had just straightened himself up. He had two rabbits slung over his shoulder, and his big bag seemed to contain many more. I walked towards him to have a look at what he was doing, and I found him manœuvring with a great steel trap.

When he had finished, we dropped into conversation in that easy way proper to wild places where few men ever come. I noticed his build and his face. His rough bonnet covered his forehead, but I could see he had plenty of thick brown hair. His eye was blue like tempered steel, and shone with a steady gleam from under projecting brows. His mouth was beautifully shaped, and his lips were full and resolute. For the rest, he was built like an ordinary dalesman— broad and flat in the shoulders, lean in the flank, and strong of limb. His clothing was coarse and poor, and his hands were rough and very red.

I said, " What takes you out at this time of the morning ? "

" Oh ! I was just lookin' round the traps. My father rents the hills from here to the Clough, and I work with him."

" You find it chilly work this weather ? "

" It's grey and cold ; but we haven't to mind those things."

" Are you busy all day ? "

" No. I only go to the traps twice, and then drive the rabbits into the town, and the rest o' the time I'm clear."

" Then where do you live ? "

" I stop by myself mostly in the wooden house at the Poachers' Hollow, and old Betty Winthrop comes and does what's wanted to keep the place right."

We walked on exchanging small talk until we came to the hollow, and I saw the tiny hut where my new friend lived. The hollow was a gruesome place. It acted as a kind of funnel whereby the wind from the great woods was poured over the beach, and sent moaning away across the sea. In summer it was gay with bracken, and golden ragwort, and wild geranium, but in winter it looked only fit for adventurous witches to gambol in.

I said, " The wind must yell awfully here when it is a gusty night."

A curious look came into the young fellow's eye, and gave me a new interest in him. He answered :

" I like it. The wind here's like nowhere else. It plays tunes on the trees there as it comes through, and I get the echoes of them. Sometimes I hear the men's voices, and then I know what it is. It's the old Norsemen going out over the sea to look at their tracks again. Bless you, I've heard them talk about the Swan's bath. Sometimes the dead ladies come and whisper, and I know they're walking in the woods all the time the dusk lasts."

I stared very much. This speech did not sound very sane, and yet it was uttered by a quiet young lad who looked as if he might be trusted. I thought, " Oh! Here's a kind of poet, or something of that sort," and I said, smilingly, " How do you come to know about the Norsemen, then ? "

" I have several books. I got one on a stall—a very good one about heroes. It has a lot in it about the Norsemen. If you come in you can see my books. You might have some tea. I put the kettle ready before I went out."

I stepped into the hut, and found it warm and cosy. A cake of barley bread was on the table, and a little black teapot stood there also. There was no furniture but a low wooden bed, one chair, a settle, and a broad shelf. On the shelf was a slate scrabbled all over with geometrical figures, and one of these figures was a parabola with two tangents drawn touching. This puzzled me much. I sat down to warm my hands and my half-frozen face, and when I felt comfortable I said,

" Do you read conic sections, young gentleman ? "

His bonnet was off now, and I saw his broad, compact forehead and his massive temples. He looked capable of reading anything.

He replied, quite simply :

" Oh, yes! I read geometrical conics."

" And did you teach yourself ? "

" Yes. It isn't hard after you've got over the sixth book of Euclid."

I grew more and more puzzled and interested. We had some tea, which made me feel positively luxurious, and then I looked at the backs of the books. There were " The Pilgrim's Progress " and " Tappan on the Will." Then came Shakespeare, a shilling edition of Keats, Drew's " Conic Sections," Hall's " Differential Calculus," Baker's " Land Surveying," Carlyle's " Heroes," a fat volume of Shelley, " The Antiquary," White's " Selborne," Bonnycastle's " Algebra," and five volumes of " The Tales of the Borders."

" You have a capital lot of books, my man. I suppose you know them all by heart, pretty well ? "

" Yes, I know them ; not by heart exactly, but I've had a lot of time these two winters, and I've gone over them and written about them."

" Well, which do you like best of all ? "

"My fancy's all for mathematics, but I like poetry."

"Ah! And I suppose you write poetry—don't you, now?"

He was not abashed—he said in an ordinary tone, "Very often. It doesn't seem good, but I go on at it. It pleases me and puts away the time now and then. There's some in that copy-book at your side."

I know what a fearful thing youthful poetry is, and I felt a discreet dread. But I opened the book and saw that the young man had been writing verses in a large strong hand. I did not read much. There was one pair of broken quatrains which I remember:—

> " Though toil is heavy I'll not be sad,
>   I'll rest content while my pulses beat;
> If I work, and love, and trust and be glad,
>   Perchance the world will come to my feet.
> But if no fortune ever be mine,
>   If my bones on this grey hill-side must lie,
> As long as I breathe I'll not repine.
>   I've gladly lived and I'll gladly die."

"You're not very particular about the form of your verses," said I.

"No! I never count syllables. I only go by accents."

"Um! Well. I shall meet you again, and you shall come and see me."

All that winter I was secluded. Day after day broke with wild weather. Sometimes the snow came and laid all the bracken under its gentle coverlid. Sometimes the wind came in from the sea, and as the mad squalls tore off the crests of the breakers, our cottage was smothered with yellow foam. I liked to go along to the wooden hut and sit with my young friend, although the tramp back in the chill darkness was not always very safe. He used also to visit me, and I lent him books. He was much taken with Burke, and would talk with a solemn enthusiasm when I encouraged him to speak about the American war and the Revolution. He began to try prose writing during this same winter, and I sometimes read his attempts. After he had shown me some quiet fragments, describing his own daily work, I advised him not to trouble himself with verse any more, and he went on imitating his favourite prose writers with curious persistence.

February came in, bringing worse weather than ever. One night the wind rose so that by nine o'clock it was hardly possible to stand in the open. The sky was like iron, and the dull red which had appeared in the West at sundown changed to a cold, neutral dimness. The birds were in great trouble, the gulls especially wailing with a peevish sharpness that made the skin creep. I looked out twice into the roaring darkness, and could see nothing except the flash of the "white horses" as they trampled and reared far out at sea. The fire was better than that wild company, so I sat a little, and then slept. A loud knocking awaked me, and, going to the door, I found that the dawn had come, and that my young friend was there.

" What is the matter ?"

" Get dressed, sir. There's bad work coming, the gale's worse, and there's a brig trying to work north.

He'll never get round the point.   You go nor'ard and rouse the Hundalee men, and I'll go south and rouse the chaps at the Bay.   Good-bye."

When I got out the wind hit me so that I had to turn and gasp a second for breath.   It seemed as though the sea were going to invade the land.   There was not a vestige of black or green water for half a mile from the beach.   Nothing but wild masses of angry whiteness coiling and winding and shivering themselves against each other.   Twice the wind stopped me as I fought my way north, and once I had fairly to lie down in a hollow until a shrieking blast gave me leave to step on.   But I got to the village and told the men, and a dozen strong fellows went back with me.   There was no lifeboat within eight miles, so we harnessed two horses to a pair of the ordinary wheels used to launch herring-boats after the winter is over, and we took one of the smaller sort of trouting-boats with us.

When we reached the Point the men from the south were there, and my young friend was among them.   All were excited, for the brig was fighting her way still through the awful sea.   She would not bear enough sail to steady her in the least, and she could only claw her way inch by inch to the northeast.

The Point was a long sandy spit, which sloped gradually away into deep water.   If the vessel could weather it, she might get away to the north, but she had gone too far into the bay, and the fishermen saw that she must choose between going ashore on the rocks of the bay and hitting the Point.   In the latter event the vessel might hold for a while before the seas finally smashed her.

The brig rose sometimes on the cross seas until we could see her copper. Then she would seem to strike savagely at the driving mist as her masts lashed forward; then she would lurch to leeward, and lie for a few horrible seconds as though she never would rise again. It could not last. My young friend said :

" Let's get the coble down to the water's edge."

The volleys of wind and the thunder of water had frightened the horses, and they stood trembling and cowed. The men had to let the boat slide down the grassy channel, which was, as it were, bevelled in the low bulge of the Point.

They had not long to wait. The brig suddenly came round, as though her helm had been put hard up.

" Rudder's gone," said one of the fishermen.

Sea after sea struck the vessel astern, and threatened to swamp her, but she managed always to shake herself. She came on like a cork that is rushed down a gutter by a shower, only giving a roll and going yard-arm under as cross-seas hit her.

At last she stopped.

" Touched," said one of the men.

But she rose again and lumbered yet a few yards forward. Then she beat herself heavily, and the next sea doubled clean over her.

" We can't do nothin', chaps. The coble winnot get two yards till she's over."

This came from the oldest fisherman.

" Oh ! for Christ's sake, let's shove off," said my young student, clasping his hands. He was pale,

and his eyes shone, as they always did when he was
excited.

"It's very well to say shove off, my bonny man,
but look at it! We brought the boat for fear there
might be a chance, but there's no chance at all."

"I think we might just have a try," said a large,
grave man. "Will three o' you come, and I'll steer
her myself?"

"I'll be one," said a stiff little man, known as
"Catfish."

"Let me go," said the young rabbit-catcher.

"I can pull as well as ever a one of you," he
pleaded, when the large man looked doubtful. I
wanted to go, but it was decided that a fisherman
would pull better than I. So we got the boat hurled
through the smother of foam, and presently we heard
the "Crack, crack," as the vanguard of the real
water began to strike at her.

My youngster was pulling with his hat off, and I
saw him now and then, as the boat swooped upward,
and hung almost perpendicularly on the striped side
of a travelling wave. I believe I prayed. An old
man, whose son was rowing the stern oar (cobles only
need three oars, two on one side, and a long one
astern) said, "Lord, have mercy on you, my bonny
Harry." Then he sobbed once, and his face became
fixed, like a mask of carven stone.

I do not know how long the wild buffeting lasted,
but I know that presently the bows of the boat appeared returning over a doubling sea, and as she
made her downward flight I saw a black, huddled
mass in her.

Then there was a rush, and the coble came up on the sand. Only one trip was needed. Five men were brought ashore; the other two hands had been taken overboard by one sea just before the ship lost her rudder.

Years went by, and I returned to dwell in cities. One evening I went to dine at a club. I was lounging in the reading-room, when a splendid-looking man attracted my attention. He was a magnificently-built young fellow, with a fine beard, and bright, steel-blue eyes. When he rose, I saw that he was perfectly dressed, and when he spoke to a waiter, his voice seemed deep, and his accent fine.

I looked down at my paper, and I then felt that he was looking at me. When I looked up, he had risen, and was looking steadily in my face. He made a step forward.

" Pardon me. How very, very strange ! " I said ; " I'm at a loss to remember you. You'll forgive me."

" Don't you remember the Poachers' Hollow, and the brig, and Burke, and the Differential ?"

Then I knew, and we shook hands heartily. We dined together, and he told me how his change of fortune had come about.

" It all came through that shipwreck," he explained.

" How was that ?"

" Well, directly I got home and changed, I sat down and wrote an account of the whole concern in some very gaudy prose, and I drove the pony into the town and handed the letter in at the " Sentinel " office. My account was printed. Old Mr. Willits—you remember him—sent to the editor to know who had done it, and then sent for me. He was very grumpy and crusty at first, but I explained my position to him simply, and he got very good humoured. He sent me to a tutor for two years and a half; then I won a Trinity scholarship, and scored two or three other things; then I went to the University, and slogged like a slave. Mr. Willits helped me. I did very well in the Tripos—not so well as men who started younger—but still I landed ninth. Now I'm principal of the new college that ——— endowed, and I have a very good thing indeed."

So my friend, the rabbit-catcher, became a successful man, and, I am sure, I wished him joy.

THE GIANTS.

IN passing along the shores of the bay, on evenings
when the water was smooth, you could hear a succession of dull thuds like the sound of distant guns.
Looking to eastward you saw a dark semicircular
streak on the water, and inside this streak a coble
glided slowly hither and thither. One man rowed
gently, letting his oars drop into the water with a
slight splash, that could be heard nevertheless a long
way off. The sweeps were so long that the rower
could not scull in the ordinary way, but crossed his
arms and held the handle of the right sweep in his
left hand, and *vice versâ*. In the stern of the boat
stood a man of gigantic size. At intervals he heaved up
a great tiller into the air and brought it down with all
his strength ; he then gathered himself for another
effort while the split end of the tiller floated on the
water ; then came another strong muscular effort, and
then another resounding splash. If the boat drew
near the brown rocks the blows of the tiller would
startle a piper or a curlew ; a long note of warning
would pierce the stillness, and a wailing answer came
from the next point ; then a shrill clamour passed all
round the bay, and the birds skimmed towards the
island like flights of dark arrows.

The black streak on the water was made by the cork floaters of a net, for the men in the coble were engaged in catching sea-trout. When the tide has flowed for some time, there is a general stir among the fish. First the dainty gobies come forward as vanguard; then come the pretty fish that the men call sea-minnows; then the dark shadows of the flounders fly swiftly over the sandy floor, and the dogcrabs sidle along in a very lively manner. As the foam creeps further and further in the larger fishes come from the deep water. Great congers with their ugly manes and villanous eyes wind in and out the rocky channels, committing assaults on smaller fishes as they come. The red rock cod leaves his stony hollows and swims over the sandy places, looking for soft crabs, or for his favourite food, the luscious crass. Last of all comes the beautiful sea-trout, skirmishing forward with short rushes, and sometimes making a swirl near the surface of the water. The fishermen wait until they think the trout have had time to reach the inner rocks, and then softly paddle the coble away from the shore. The net is dexterously shot, and a good man can manage to do this without making a splash. The long curtain is about four feet deep, and lead sinkers make it hang true. Not a word is spoken until the great bladder which marks the end of the net falls into the sea. Then the boat is taken toward the shore, and the fishermen rest quiet for awhile, until it is time to begin splashing. The big pole is dashed into the water in order to frighten the trout towards the net, and very great judgment is required in the rower, for if he happens to take the wrong track he may easily put the fish in the way of escape.

The gigantic man who used to ply the tiller, and the old rower, were both very clever at this kind of fishing. The elder of the two was called " Big Harry," and the younger was called " Little Harry." There was humour in this mode of naming, for Little Harry stood six feet four, while Big Harry only measured about six feet three. Big Harry had four sons altogether, and the average height of the family was about six feet four. All the lads were extremely good-looking, but the old man liked Little Harry best, and always took him for partner. The other sons handled the second of the family cobles, and the five men made an excellent living. It was a fine sight to see the fellows go away in the afternoon. They wore great boots that came up to the thigh, blue woollen caps, or sou-westers, and thick dark Guernseys. All of them were dark-haired and dark-eyed, and with their earrings, they looked strange and foreign. The three younger lads, who were much bigger than their father, went partners in one boat, and the two gaudy craft took their several ways. The men never said good-bye or good-night, nor did they use any other form of politeness, because by the fishermen any demonstration of friendliness, even among relations, is counted as showing softness. The mother of the lads was a handsome, broad-shouldered woman who had been a beauty in her day. She mostly used to spare time for seeing her tall fellows off, but she never waved to them. In spite of this reticence, it must not be supposed that the family were

unkindly : more gentle and helpful men never lived,
and there was not one of them who had not done
some brave thing It may be worth while to tell a
story illustrative of their disposition.

One brisk morning, when the sea was running high,
a little boy was sailing a fine model yacht in one of
the great pools on the shore.   The tide was running
in, and presently the advancing water rushed into the
pool.   The yacht was just in the centre when the
whirl of the sea took her.   She swung round ; the
westerly wind caught her, and in a moment she was
over the barrier and away into deep water.   The little
thing was well leaded, and she went off like a dolphin.
The youthful owner saw her now and again as she
topped the waves, and he lamented exceedingly.   At
last it struck him to run north to the village.   Just as
he reached the cove, Big Harry's younger sons were
coming in after a night at sea.   The men were wet
and sleepy enough, but when the little boy told them
his story they lifted him into the bow of the coble
and shoved off again.   With three reefs in the sail
they dodged out among the jumping seas, and ran
over the bay after the truant yacht.   The swift coble
soon overhauled the runaway, and the men came
back well drenched by their second trip.   The whole
thing was done with perfect simplicity ; and the fishermen would not accept even a glass of ale from the
boy's father.   They said " they were glad to see the
bairn so pleased," and they tease the said "bairn"
about his skill in navigation even to this day.   When
we see kindness like this we may be content to do
without words or other minor demonstrations.

During all the long nights Big Harry and Little Harry used to sit together very silently. Sometimes when the corks at one part of the net went under water suddenly, one of the men would say, " There's a troot fast," but conversation did not extend beyond elementary observations like this. The dark came down over the bay, and the last gleam died away from the distant hills. The water purred softly with little treble sounds against the sides of the boat; the trees made hoarse noises, and sometimes the long whistle of an otter (who is also a trout fisher) would come from the shaggy sides of the brown stream. The men sat on amid the mystery of the night, but they had no care for the picturesque. By-and-by the time for a haul would come, and the muscular fish were pitched " flopping " into the basket. Then the nets were shot again, and the resonant splashing begun. If the tide suited, the boat stayed on till dawn. As soon as the cushats began to fly from the woods to the fields, and the hillsides were streaked with grey motes of light, Big Harry and his son rowed into the cove, and then Little Harry went to catch the old mare on the moor. A boy drove the night's fish to the station, and Big Harry slept heavily in the dark box bed.

Father and sons led this life for many years. Their only change came when the herring shoals moved southward, and then the five strong men used to make a great deal of money. They saved too, and were much better off than some people who live in finer houses. Indeed, they had much need to earn a great deal, for those great frames were not easily kept up.

Big Adam once ate five eggs after his return from a night's fishing. He then inquired "When will breakfast be ready?" So it will be seen that his appetite was healthy.

It seemed that nothing but gradual decay could ever sap the strength of any one of these fine athletes, yet a miserable mischance made a break in the family, and changed Big Harry into a sorrowful man. He came ashore one rainy morning, and he and his son had sore work in hauling the coble up. There was no one to drive the fish to the station, so Little Harry volunteered. It was a long drive for such a bad day, and when the young man came home he was chilled. He shivered a good deal and could not sleep, but no one dreamed of bringing a doctor for a man with a forty-seven inch chest. Within a very short while Little Harry was taken by rapid consumption, and succumbed like a weakling from the town. On the day of the funeral the father would not follow the coffin over the moor. He lay with his face pressed on the pillow, and the bed shook with his sobbing. He never would take another son for mate, because he thought he might distress the lad if he showed signs of comparing him with the dead. He preferred a stranger. He liked carrying Little Harry's son about, and he used to be pleased when the clergyman said to the child, "Well, and how is your big pony?"— the pony being the grandfather. When the lad grew big enough to handle the small-sized plasher the old man took him as partner, and he boasts about the little fellow's cleverness.

THE COLLIER SKIPPER.

MANY old-fashioned people who read of the massacres caused by steamboat collisions, think regretfully of the time when eight hundred sail of ships would make the trip between Tyne and Thames without so much as the loss of a bowsprit from one of the fleet. It was slow work, perhaps, and it might be a tedious sight (say those who praise past times), to see a ship being hauled up the river foot by foot with a warp and a kedge; yet we do not get cheap coals now, for all our science, and we have lost our seamen. The old inhabitants of the eastern seaports never cease to lament the progress of steam. They point out that all the money made in the brig colliers goes into few hands, and is carried away to be spent in London and Torquay, and Cannes, and Paris, by the great coalowners. They say, too, that the new race of seamen are unsocial beings who do no good to any town that the steamers run from. The modern "hand" comes into the river, say, at dusk; sees his vessel put under the coal spout, jumps ashore to buy a loaf and a few herrings, and then goes off to sea by three in the morning. This goes on all the year round, and if the sailor gets four-and-twenty hours to spend at home, he thinks himself wonderfully lucky.

The sailor-men of old times seldom worked in the winter. All the colliers were laid up in the river, and the men lived on their summer earnings, so that multitudes of small tradesmen, who are now unable to live, fared very comfortably then.

These complaints may not be very logical or well founded, but the people who make them speak with perfect belief. Whatever may be thought of the social aspect of the question, the nautical aspect is not to be mistaken; for our school of seamen is undoubtedly departed.

The old collier sailor was a man of one faculty : he could handle a ship to perfection, but he could do nothing else, and he knew nothing else. On shore he was a child of the most innocent description, and the world that lay outside the regular line traversed by his old black tub, was a place beyond his conception. It is true that he sometimes went to such far-off regions as the Baltic, but even that extent of travel failed to open his mind. The worthy man who said that the four quarters of the globe were " Russia, Prussia, Memel, and Shields," was the type of the travelled collier captain. It is hardly possible to understand the complete ignorance of some of those fine sailors, or to conceive the methods on which they worked their ships. A man who could neither read nor write would take his vessel without a mistake from port to port. The lights on the coast were his only books, and his one intellectual exercise consisted in calculating the set of the ebb and the flood. With all the phenomena that he was used to observe in his ordinary life, he could deal promptly and sagaciously,

but anything new tended to disarrange his mind.
When steamers were first ordered to carry red and
green side-lights with a high white light hung forward,
an old captain saw the mysterious coloured circles
coming down on him. He did not understand this
new thing, and his faculties became confused. He
shouted " Hard a-starboard. We 'll be into a chemist's
shop." This momentary infirmity of purpose was the
source of much fun among more advanced mariners in
his town. Another master who happened to have a
leisure evening went to hear a popular astronomical
lecture. He was much troubled by what he heard, and
he explained his perplexity with great feeling to his
friends. He said : " The man told the lot of us that
the world turned round and round; but I cannot see
how that can be. The Hatter's Rock's been there
ever since I can mind." It sometimes happened that
a captain more than usually competent was sent over
seas to strange regions. One gentleman who could
read and use a chart was despatched to Rotterdam.
After getting over the bar and well away to the east,
he produced his charts and made a learned inspection ;
but the charts had been a long time in the lockers,
and circumstances combined to alarm him extremely.
He went up on deck and called to his mate, " Put her
about, the rats has eaten Holland." One of the most
remarkable of the old school was a man who could
actually take his ship about and find his place on the
chart without being able to read the names himself.
He always became very shortsighted on longish
voyages. Towards the end of his time the new race
of apprentices who had learned to read began to go to

sea: before that period he had only been used to
coasting trips, and the learned youths were a godsend
to him when his owners sent him far afield. He
would call his lad down below, and, assuming a tender
air, would give the seasoned youngster a glass of rum.
He would then point to the chart and say, " We're
there. What is that place, my man? I can't see very
well." On receiving his answer, he would remark,
gravely, "I thought it was that." This innocent
device gave the greatest entertainment to his irreve-
rent pupils. Sometimes this kind of ignorance led to
complications. One old gentleman bored away
through a fog for several days under the pleasing
impression that he was going north about from
Liverpool. After a long time a vessel came past and
the lost captain inquired, "Are we going right for
the Castle foot?" The stranger made answer.
"What Castle foot?" Whereupon the incensed
skipper said, "There's only one Castle foot. Tynemouth Castle." The answer was discouraging: "If
you go as you're going, you'll be at Newfoundland in
a very short time." This hero felt his way back and
after many days and much hailing of passing ships he
sighted St. Abb's Head. He then said with pride,
"Ah! here's England. Aw thowt aw would fetch
her." He had really known no more of his route
than a player at blind man's buff knows of his way
about a room.

Of course very many of the captains were more
accomplished than the stolid persons concerning
whom so many droll legends still linger; but the
fact remains, that valuable property and valuable lives

were entrusted to men who wrought solely by rule of
thumb, and that the trust was, on the whole, very
wisely bestowed. With clumsy old craft that sailed
in heavy weather as though they were dragging an
anchor at the bottom, and that missed stays on the
faintest provocation, these men carried goods to the
value of millions, without incurring nearly the loss
which is borne through the failure of the smart iron
steamers. They are nearly all gone now, and the
public are not much the better. Many good judges
think that in the event of a great naval war we shall
feel the need of that fine recruiting ground that lay
between Spittal and Yarmouth. The old collier
sailor, illiterate as he was, and stupid as he was in
many respects, made a model man-of-war's man when
he had been drilled into shape. He was alert, obe-
dient, and utterly careless of danger; he had the
fighting instinct developed to the point of ferocity;
he was at once strong and docile, and his very simplicity made him the best possible instrument to be
employed on dangerous enterprises. The last specimens will soon be beyond the reach of social students.
Here and there may be found some bronzed old man
who remembers when the Tyne was little more than a
ditch flooded at tide-time. He hobbles sturdily to
the pier and looks at the passing vessels with dim
eyes. The steamers pass up and down with their
swaggering turmoil; the little tugs whisk the sailing
ships deftly in and out; but he will always think that
the world was better when the bar was shallow, and
when the sailors worked up stream without the aid of
those unseamanlike kettles.

IN THE BAY.

THE screw steamer "Coquet" left a little port on the north coast early one October. She was bound for Genoa; and as this was a long trip, a little group of men, among whom were several who owned shares in her, waved their farewells from the end of the pier. A number of small tradesmen and a few well-to-do fishermen had formed a company to buy her, so she was regarded as quite an institution of the port. A smart captain had managed her cleverly, and she paid, during five years, an average dividend of nearly fifty per cent., after the modest claims of the " managing " owner had been satisfied. Naturally she was regarded as a treasure, and her fortunate owners used to make triumphant observations about her to less lucky men. The steamer had gone through some very bad weather; but as every rivet in her hull had been examined while she was being put together, and that too by a man whom no skulker could deceive, she had lived in seas that sent scamped ships to the bottom.

The "Coquet" got away down Channel and struck for Ushant without any mishap; but when she got well into the Bay the sky began to look ominous. On the second morning the sea ran very strong, and by midday the gale had fairly come. All the fine descriptions of heavy weather in the Bay help one but little to understand what it is really like. It is hardly possible to think coherently about the enormous hurly-burly, much less to write or speak so as to make anyone understand how the masses of water move and how they sound. The "Coquet" got into a very bad quarter indeed, and the captain soon saw that it was useless to try running her. All hands were warned; the formalities of watches were dispensed with; and the engineers received orders to get on every possible ounce of steam. Then the ship was placed with her head to the sea, and the master took his place on the bridge. He did not know what a very long spell he would have. Only by keeping the engines at full speed ahead the vessel was enabled to hold her ground, and sometimes when the usual eight great waves were followed by the mountainous ninth, she lost considerably. The captain had to watch like a cat; for an instant's nervousness, a momentary failure of judgment, would have let her come round, and then all would have been soon over. The men hung on anyhow, and the two hands at the wheel were lashed, for the hull was seldom above water. A pouring stream rushed over the steamer; and hardly had one volume of water passed away when another came down like thunder. There was very little of the usual creamy foam, for the sea ran over the ship as though she were not there. When the downward flights came, the captain on the high bridge was often up to his knees in water; and again and again he made up his mind that his vessel could never come out of it. Once, when the mate

dodged aft and clambered to the bridge, the "Coquet"
took a long rush down, after she had reared on end like
a horse. Her plunge was like the dive of a whale,
and the screw "raced"—that is, whirled round high
above the sea-level. The mate said, "She's gone,
sir;" the captain replied, "Give her time." Once
more she came up and shook herself; but it seemed as
though her elasticity was gone. In truth, her deck
had an ugly slant. During all this time the wind was
growing, and the sea was gaining speed and strength.
It could not very well last, and nobody knew that
better than the captain. A blinding scuffle of cross-seas
came and the "Coquet" was smothered for a while;
the captain heard a crashing sound, and when he looked
round the starboard boat was smashed and hanging in
splinters, while the port boat was torn clean away.
These were the only two boats that the vessel had. The
slant or "list" grew more pronounced, for the cargo
had shifted; and the steamer was now like a boxer
whose left hand is tied behind his back. She seemed
to take the blows passively, only lungeing doggedly
up when the wild welter had flowed over her, and still
keeping her nose to the sea. All night long the captain
hung on the bridge. It was his second night, and in
that time he had only had one biscuit, that the mate
gave him. His legs were very tired, and every muscle
was strained in the effort to cling fast. He could, of
course, see nothing; and it was only by the compass
that he could tell how to keep her head. At midnight
a wave swept everything; the compass amidships and
the one astern both went, and a man was taken overboard. Still the wind kept on, and the only light to

be seen was the flash of the curling spray. The dawn broke, and still the sea was bad. At seven o'clock a tremendous crash sounded, and the vessel staggered: there was a long ripping grind, and the port bulwark was gone; so all the seas that came aboard after this had their own way, and as the vessel "listed" to port the deck was a very dangerous place. The mate managed again to get near the captain. He said: "The men want you to put her before the sea, sir; so do I." The captain replied: "If you propose such a thing again, sir, I'll break your head as soon as I can get loose from here. Keep the men in heart." At noon the second mate came forward with a white face, saying: "The tarpaulin's gone off the after-hold, sir." The captain was badly put out by hearing this, but he shouted: "Lash the men how you can, and try to make fast again." While the men (with ropes round their waists) were wrestling with the tarpaulin, a wave doubled over the ship, making her shake; and, as the captain after-wards said, "the fellows were swimming like black-beetles in a basin of water." One poor "ordinary" went overboard in the wash of this sea, and nothing could be done for him. At four o'clock the chief engineer came up, and managed to tell the captain that two fires were drowned out, and that the firemen would stay below no longer. The captain asked, "Have you the middle fire?" and receiving an affirmative answer, he said, "Give the men each half a tumbler of brandy to put some pluck in them." A merry Irish fireman was so influenced by his dose of spirit that he joked and coaxed his mates down below again, and once more the fight was resumed. The sun drooped low,

and threw long swords of light through rifts in the
dull grey veil. The captain knew it was now or never,
so he managed to get the men called where they could
hear him, and shouted: "Now, when that sun dips
we'll have the warmest half-hour of all. If she lives
through that and the gale breaks, I can save her. If
she doesn't, you must die like men. You should say
your prayers." When the "warm half-hour" came it
was something beyond belief. The "Coquet" was as
bare as a newly launched hull before it was over; then
came a kind of long sigh, and the wind relaxed its
force. All night the sea lessened; and at dawn there
was but a light air of wind, with no breaking waves at
all. The captain then dared to run before the sea; he
got his vessel round, and she went comfortably away
on the steady roll. He had known all along that if he
tried to fetch her round she would assuredly share the
fate of the "London." That steamer was smashed in
by a doubling sea that came over her stern while the
captain was trying to take her about.

The master of the "Coquet" had been seventy-two
hours on the bridge, and he was nearly asleep as he
walked. In trying to get to his berth he fell face foremost, and slept on the cabin-floor in his wet oilskin suit.
When he woke he had a nastier problem than ever, for
his compasses were gone, and the ship had a dangerous
"list." However, he soon bethought him of a tiny
pocket-compass which he had in his state-room.
Working with this, and managing to get a sight of
the sun, he contrived to get within fourteen miles of
Gibraltar—which was very fair seamanship. He
reached Genoa; but the ship was sixteen days overdue,

and the people at home were alarmed. On the morning after the "Coquet's" arrival one of her owners looked through a local journal, and, finding no good news, went and got his shares under-written 60 per cent. more. On coming out of the office he was met by a friend, who heartily congratulated him on his good luck. When he asked wherein the good luck consisted, he was shown a paragraph in another local journal which stated that "The steamship 'Coquet' arrived at Genoa, sixteen days overdue. Boats gone, port bulwark gone, compasses gone, and two men lost overboard."

The lesson to be learned from the "Coquet's" escape is simple. In that very gale as many men were killed at sea as would have fallen in a moderately important battle. The number of missing steamers was great, and there is no doubt but that most of these vessels foundered. The "Coquet" was built under the eye of a critic who did not suffer champagne to bias his ideas of solid workmanship. She is still earning heavy dividends for her owners. The steamers that broke in two and went down were not superintended on the stocks by a shrewd and vigilant overlooker: so they drowned their crews.

THE SIBYL.

AN old woman lived in a one-roomed cottage among the sandhills bordering the sea. Her place was only a hut with thatched roof and stone floor, but coals were plentiful, so Mary was able to make herself very comfortable. The wind made a great noise with moaning and shrieking among the bents, but Mary was not learned enough in romantic literature to be moved by weird sounds. She did not like to hear a fox howl on the hill, because that woful cry boded ill fortune ; but the tumult of ordinary winter evenings never affected her. All day she crouched over her fire, filling her pipe at intervals with coarse tobacco, and smoking sedately. She did not look up when people entered, for her sight was dim ; yet she knew the tread and the voice of every lad in the village who had once been in her company, and she very rarely made mistakes in bestowing her greetings. Her face was like a walnut-shell, so deep and intricate were the creases in her brown skin; and the broad outlines of her features were massive and strong. At the end of the last century she had been a strapping girl with a fine gait, and she liked to tell how the young Squire used to admire her, and how he stopped his horse and spoke with her by the wayside. The young Squire had grown

into an old man, but Mary always remembered him as
he was when he cantered through the village on his
croptailed roadster, and displayed his brass buttons
and his neat buckskins for the admiration of the fisher-
girls. No one knew how old Mary was : she herself
fixed her age at "about a thousand," but even those
who believed in her most regarded this estimate as
exaggerated. She always spoke of the Squire as being
younger than herself, and as she was still living when
he was within five years of one hundred, she must have
been very old indeed. Her chance allusions to past
events were startling. She could remember the talk
of her own grandmother, and when she repeated things .
which she had heard as a child, it seemed as though a
dim light had been thrown on antiquity. She liked
to speak about a mysterious French privateer that had
landed men who "went and set up their gob to old
Mrs. Turnbull at the Bleakmoor Farm, and tyok every
loaf oot o' the pantry;" but no one could ever tell
what privateer she meant. She had heard about
Bonaparte, and she remembered when Big Meg, the
village cannon, was brought down to the cliff and
planted ready for invaders. Her grandmother had ,
spoken often of the time when all the men from the
Ratcliffe property, away west, had followed somebody
that wanted to send the King away, but Mary's knowledge of this circumstance was severely indefinite.
The lads in the place would have followed their Squire
had he chosen to imitate "Ratcliffe," but the Squire
of that day was a quiet man who liked the notion of
keeping his head on his shoulders. Mary knew of
one country beyond England, and she conceived that

Englishmen were meant to thrash the inhabitants of
that country on all possible occasions : beyond this
her knowledge of Europe and the globe did not extend.   Her function in the village was that of story-
teller, and her house was a place of meeting for all the
lads.   She taught aspiring youths to smoke, and this
harmful educational influence she supplemented by
teaching her pupils many wild stories of a ghostly
character.   Her own sons had been four in number ;
one of them survived as an old one-armed man ; the
others were drowned.   But when Mary got her little
school of listeners about her, she said it made her feel
" as if Tom and the other bairns were back agyen."
Smart lads used to leave the village and come back
after many days with flat caps and earrings, and a
sailorly roll.   Mary would say, " That should be
Harry's Tommy, by the voice.   Is that so, hinny ? "
and when Harry's Tommy answered " Yes," Mary
would say, " Your awd pipe's on the top o' the oven ;
sit thee doon and give us your cracks."   Mary's
pupils all had pipes which were kept on the oven-top
for them, and she was much distressed if she found
that anyone smoked a pipe belonging to a lad who had
been drowned.   When the school gathered in the dark
evenings, Mary liked to scold a little about the decay
of manly spirit.   In her time the men used to watch
at night till the low black lugger stole into the bay.
Then some discreet farmer would hear a trampling of
horses in his stables, and if in the morning Bet and
Ball and Matchem were splashed a good deal, and
tired, there was always the keg of sound spirits at the
kitchen door or in one of the mangers.   Mary had

often gone down the north road and up the Dead Man's Trail to listen for the Preventive men, and she spoke with glee of the fun, for she had been swift of foot, and her imitation of the Jenny Howlet's cry was perfect.

The old woman liked to frighten her hearers. She knew that most of the villagers believed profoundly in ghosts and bogles, and she was never so well pleased as when she knew that not one of her school cared for going home alone. Old George, the organist, had once seen the white lady from the tower, but he could not be induced to tell his experience. George's musical duties were restricted to turning a handle, for the tunes played by the organ were put in on separate rollers, and thus the musician's function was limited. But the fishermen regarded him as a fine player, and he did not care to imperil a serious reputation by telling frivolous ghost stories. So Mary, who had heard the story long ago from George's own lips, did duty as narrator :—

George was coming through the woods on a dark night. He came to a part of the walk where the path makes a descent to a hollow shaded by thick, arching branches. Suddenly (said Mary) George's collie ran back howling, and tried to snuggle its head under its master's coat. George patted the beast and laid him down, but the dog still clung about his master's feet, and moaned. George turned the poor animal round, and tried to force him forward. The collie gave one very loud cry, and died. Then George became mysteriously cold, and presently he saw a lady standing among the shrubs. She waved to him, and

he saw that her eyes were white; then she moved
through the trees and passed away. The sceptical
shepherd said that the collie had eaten some phos-
phorus which had been spread for the rats, but Mary
never gave this prosaic explanation. She and George
believed that the dog died of fright, and that the
grave organist had seen the lady from the tower, so
many youths grew up believing that the grim square
building was haunted.

On one night of 1859, Mary had told some of her
stories with much effect. A gale was blowing from
the east, and the hoarse roar of the wind sounded very
strangely. The "school" was in the goose-skinned
condition which must be attained by all who wish to
catch the true flavour of a ghost story. There came a
scraping sound at the door, and a gasping moan. The
lads huddled together and dared not look round. The
moan was repeated, and Mary ordered one of her
pupils to go at once and open the door. But discipline
was forgotten, and the young gentleman who was
deputed to solve the mystery stayed open-mouthed in
his seat. The old woman hobbled to the door, and
found a man lying on his face. The poor fellow was a
Portuguese sailor. He had swum through the surf
from a vessel that was hard-and-fast on the rocks
below the house, and it was his last exhausted
effort that startled the assembly of youths. Mary
told this story (with supernatural additions) until her
death.

There are captains, mates, and sailor-men in all
parts of the world who remember the old story-teller,
for it is pretty certain that her influence had a good

deal to do with sending many a tall fellow away southward to the great seaports in quest of adventures. Her cottage is still standing, but a sulky hind reigns there, and the unique collection of pipes is dispersed.

A VOLUNTEER LIFE-BRIGADE.

THERE is generally very heavy weather in winter time on the north-east coast. From North Sunderland the Farne Islands can hardly be seen, for the tumultuous waves in the narrow channels throw up clouds of spray. At the mouth of the Tyne the sea runs strongly, and the great piers have to meet endless charges of green masses that break on the stonework and pour along the footway in foaming streams. As the evening comes, knots of men stroll toward the pier. They are all clothed in thick guernseys and business-like helmets, and on their breasts they have the letters V.L.B. They are the Volunteer Life Brigade. The brigade is very mixed in composition. There are carpenters, bankers, pilots, clerks, lawyers, tradesmen of all grades, and working men of all trades. At the middle of the pier stands a strong wooden house, in which there is one great room where the watchmen sit, and also numerous small boxes with berths where rescued men are laid. Hot-water bottles are constantly ready, and a mysterious array of restoratives rest handy on a side-table.

Since the great piers were run out to sea the water in the Tyne has been much deepened; but this advantage has its drawback in the fact that the sea pours through the deepened channel like the swirl of a millrace.   As soon as the tiers of shipping begin to creak and moan with the lurching swell the people know that there may be bad work.   The brigadesmen sit chatting in thèir warm shed.   They know that they must go to work in the morning; they know that they may be drenched and aching in every limb before the dawn whitens : yet they take everything as it comes with cheerful stoicism. During the winter of 1880 scores of men travelled to business at Newcastle for a week at a stretch without having lain once in bed.   They went out when their services were required ; stood to their ropes, and were hustled about by the sea: they brought crew after crew ashore, and in the mornings they fared without grumbling to office or warehouse or shop.   Snatches of sleep on the hard benches made their only rest, yet they stood it out.

The stormy nights are passed much in the same way. The men who are not looking out sit smoking and gossiping ; the foam piles itself softly to the weather side of the house, and the spray falls with a keen lash-ing sound on the stones outside.   Towards the end of the pier there is nothing to be seen but a vague trouble, as though a battle were going on in the dark, and to the north the Tynemouth light throws a long shaft of brightness through the mist.   Presently a light is seen away southward or out to the east, and all the men are on the alert directly.   If a ship from the south can only weather the end of the pier and escape the wash from the north, she soon gets into the fairway, but it is not easily done in stormy weather.   The light makes long lunges and describes great arcs on the background of the darkness; then the brigadesmen know that the ship is in the stream that pours up the gulf made by the piers. If she keeps her red light open till she is nearly abreast of the House, there is only one more danger for her. She may strike on the Black Middens (a heap of snaggy rocks lying under Tynemouth), and in that case the south-side men have nothing to do with her. But sometimes the vessel shows all her lights and rushes upon the South Pier. Then the men wait for the last lurch and that wallowing crash that they know so well. The rocket is laid, and flies out over the rigging; the brigadesmen haul on their rope, and the basket comes rocking ashore along the line. It is not child's play to stand in the open and work the rocket apparatus; sometimes a whole row of men are struck by a single sea, and have to hang on wherever they can. Sometimes a careless man is carried along the pier like a cork, and sometimes one is washed clean over the side. A lucky young gentleman was taken into the sea one winter and buffeted smartly until a chance wave landed him again. The buffeting and drenching are taken as part of the day's work, and the young fellows joke about it just as soldiers will joke under fire. There is much curiosity as the basket is hauled in. On one occasion a cat and her kittens were the first rescued of a ship's company, and on another occasion a dog came ashore looking much surprised at his position. At various times all sorts and conditions of men have to slide along that friendly rope. Stolid Dutchmen, gesticulating Italians, cool north-country sailors are landed, and all are treated alike. A solemn man with a rum-bottle awaits

them as they pass into the friendly light of the House :
like some officiating priest he gravely pours out a
glassful and silently hands it to the rescued seafarer ;
then the berth and the hot-water bottle are made
ready, and the fortunate sailor is warmly wrapped up.

It sometimes happens that the rocket cannot be
used—perhaps on account of the position of the vessel,
perhaps through the stupidity of the crew.   In that
case other means must be employed.   Last winter a
ship came on the shore ; the sea broke heavily over
her, and her crew had to take to the rigging.   A
plucky brigadesman swam off through waves that might
have stupefied a bulldog ; he had to watch his chances,
and breathe when the crest had rushed on so that he
might make his next plunge through the combing
crest ; and he managed to make his rope fast and save
the people.   Southward of Shields a ship got into a
still more awkward place than the one last mentioned.
She was carried in by a terrific sea, and jammed on
the stones at the foot of a cliff.   The captain's wife
and child were lashed to the mast, and the captain
himself was made fast somewhere ; all the other poor
souls were washed overboard.   No boat could live in
the breakers ; no rocket was handy.   But a sailor
called Matthews got some friends to lower him down
the face of the scarp.   The wind knocked him against
jutting points ; the rope twirled and spun him about ;
but he got foothold on the deck and managed to hang
on.   By working cautiously he dodged up to the mast
and fastened the little child in a comfortable bight
of the rope ; then he sent the woman aloft ; then he
sent the captain, and was hauled up safely himself.

Matthews had no reward for this piece of work, and is now a poor pitman.

There is no end to the bravery of these amateur life-savers. Only a very little while ago a ship came on shore. The sea was like a huge pouring cataract, and the wind pressed like a solid body. The dandy new lifeboats were beaten back; the men on board tugged and strained till they were exhausted. The oars were double-manned, but nothing would avail; and all the time the cry of the men on the wrecked vessel sounded through the storming of the gale. At last one man said, " Let's have the old ' Tyne.' " The " Tyne " is a superannuated lifeboat which is kept under lock and key. The key was refused, and the men who demanded it were implored not to tempt Providence. Thereupon they coolly formed themselves into a phalanx, rushed against the door, burst it in, hauled the old " Tyne " down, and saved eight lives.

KEELMEN.

THE keel is a strange kind of barge which is only seen on three of our northern rivers. She is sharp at both ends, and her lines are extremely fine. When loaded her deck is flush with the water; yet, under sail, her speed is very great, and she is as handy as a skiff. These boats are principally used for carrying coals to and from vessels that lie out in the river; but they are often employed in conveying various sorts of goods from town to town. In the old times, when the Tyne was very shallow, the colliers were loaded from keels, and the river then swarmed with the low black craft. The keelmen formed a little commonwealth by themselves; their dress, their language, their customs were all peculiar, and they were like a foreign race planted among English neighbours. In the town of Shields alone there were three dialects— Keelish, Sheelish, and Coblish. The Keelish was spoken by the keelmen, Sheelish by the tradespeople, and Coblish by the pilots; but Keelish was the most remarkable of the three tongues. Its idiom, pitch, and pronunciation were so odd that nobody from south of the Wear could understand it well without long practice, any more than he could understand the social customs of the men who spoke it. The " Keel Row,"

which is the great Northumbrian song, is written in
very fair Keelish, and no south-countryman can read
the original.

The old-fashioned keelman began his week on
Saturday afternoon. He washed himself thoroughly,
and then appeared dressed in a white flannel coat
with horn buttons, loose knee-breeches, and blue
worsted stockings. He it was, and not the pitman,
who had a chaste fancy in the matter of bulldogs, and
he rather liked seeing those interesting animals fight.
He himself liked fighting too, and the keelmen's
quarter on a Saturday night used to be a very warlike
region; for champions from the various streets fought
for the honour of their respective districts, and the
women encouraged the combatants with much energy
and enthusiasm. When the new police-force was
organized, it was as much as a constable's life was
worth to venture alone into Sandgate on a Saturday
evening; but the place is more civilized now. After
the Saturday's drinking bout and incidental combat the
keelman had Sunday in which to cultivate the graces.
He lounged on the quay and made witty remarks
about the passers-by; or he strolled to the Moor, in
all the glory of flannels and gay stockings, to see a
dog-fight. When Monday came his pleasures were at
an end. His black boat was laid alongside of some
grim collier, and the baskets were plied until the keel
sank to the water-level. If there was any wind the
sail was run up, and the keel went away merrily
enough; if it was calm the sweeps had to be handled,
and the craft travelled at about one mile per hour.
The deepening of the rivers has altered the conditions

of life a good deal for the watermen; but the race is much the same in every respect as it was eighty years ago. The Saturday combats are not so violent, and the dog-fighting is a thing of the past; but the men are like their forefathers in habits and speech. The keelman has many points in common with the pitman. He is more ignorant, because his life on the water begins very early and he is isolated for the better part of every week; so he is very simple and innocent of the world's ways. His horizon is bounded by the black banks of his river. Of nature he knows nothing, excepting that rivers run into the sea, and that tides have to be watched. In the daytime he toils on the brown flood of the Tyne; and at night he still toils on the same flood, which is then lit into lurid brilliance by the fires of the low factory chimneys and furnaces. People who work on crowded water-ways seem to acquire an extraordinary proficiency in the art of abuse, and in the said art a keelman is much superior to the Thames bargeman. His collection of epithets is large, and, since he is combative by nature, he engages freely in the war of words when engagements at close quarters are impracticable. He is no respecter of persons. The most dignified captain that ever stood on the deck of a clipper is not safe from his criticism, and even her Majesty's uniform is not sacred in his eyes. A keel once drifted against the bow of a man-of-war, and the first lieutenant of the vessel inquired, " Do you know the consequences of damaging one of her Majesty's ships?" The keelman was unprepared with an answer to this problem, but with characteristic flippancy he inquired, " Div ye knaw the conseekue of a keel losin' her tide ? " The keelman's ignorance of all objects not to be seen on the river is really strange. Two worthies wanted to go on board a brig called the " Swan." The vessel had a figure-head representing the bird after which she was named, so the keelmen hailed in the following terms, " Like-a-goose-and-not-a-goose, ahoy ! " They were much disappointed by the inattention of the crew. The keelman is religious in his way, but his ideas lack lucidity. Two friends had left their keel aground up the river and were walking across a field, when they were chased by a savage bull. They fled to a tree, and the fleeter-footed man got to the first fork. The second had swarmed a fair distance up the trunk, when the bull arrived and began butting with such vigour that the tree was shaken. The climber could not get up further ; so his friend, seeing the imminent danger, said, " Canst thou pray, Geordie ? " The panting unfortunate answered, " Yes." Whereupon his mate said, " Gan on then, for he'll have thee in a minute." The bull kept on pushing the tree ; so the keelman tried a totally irrelevant supplication. He said, " For what we are about to receive may the Lord make us truly thankful." Teasing urchins sometimes shout after the keelman, " Who jumped on the grindstone ? " and this query never fails to rouse the worst wrath in the most sedate ; for it touches a very sore point. Two men were caught by a heavy freshet and driven over the bar. The legend declares that one of these mariners saw, in the dusk, a hoop floating by. The hoop was full of foam ; and with swift intuition the keelman said, " We're saved ; here's

a grindstone swimming!" He followed up his discovery by jumping on to the grindstone—with most
unsatisfactory results. His error has led to much loss
of temper among his tribe.

In the matter of sport the keelman's ideas are
narrowed to one point. He is only interested in boat-
racing; but he makes up by fervour for his want of
extended views. For weeks before a great race the
Sandgate quarter is in a state of excitement, and
wagering is general and heavy. The faith which the
genuine keelman has in his athletic idol is almost
touching. When the well-known Chambers rowed
for the championship of England in 1867, an admirer
shouted as the rower went to the starting point, " Gan
on, Bob; I've putten everything I have on you."
Chambers shook his head mournfully and said, " Take
it all off again, my man; I cannot win." But the en-
thusiast would not accept even that excellent authority.
For a long time before the last championship race the
sporting keelmen put by money every week to back
the Tynesider, and the melancholy result of the race
desolated Sandgate. Perhaps it was well that the
Englishman was beaten; for in the event of any
athletic success the whole Tyneside population become
very arrogant, and the keelmen insufferable. Each
one of them takes credit for the victory, and the community of Sandgate becomes a large mutual admiration society.

In politics the keelman's notions are crude. If a
stranger spoke disrespectfully of the present member
for Newcastle in the hearing of a keelman it is not
improbable that a crowd would be called, and the

critic would be immersed in the river : but the crowd
could not explain lucidly their reasons for such strong
political action.   The fact is that the keelman has no
interest in the affairs that occupy people ashore.   The
brown river, the set of the tides, the arrival and sailing
of the colliers, the noisy gossip of water-side characters
on Saturday night—these things fill up the measure
of his observation.   He lives out his hard-working,
hard-drinking life like the stupid Englishman he is ;
and when he dies his fights are remembered and his
prowess lauded by generous mourners.

BLOWN NORTH.

T HE brig " Wansbeck " sailed on a February day
at about four in the afternoon. She was a fine
little vessel, but very badly found in sails and running-
gear. The crew had signed for a voyage to Malmo ;
and the owner hurried the ship away because he feared
she might be " neaped " in the little river, as the
tides were taking off. The cargo was very badly
stowed ; and when the pilot came on board it was discovered that part of the pump-gear had not arrived.
The captain told the owner of this ; and that gentleman said the ship should go to sea without any pumps
at all rather than he would see her lie on the mud. So
the moorings were cast off, and the tug took the tow-
rope on board. Luckily, just as the stern-rope was
cast off, the missing pump-gear came to hand.

The sky was heavy and grey ; a snoring breeze
blew from the E.N.E., and the vessel went away on a
south-east course under double-reefed topsails and
foresail. Everything moveable about the decks was
secured, and the pumps were set on ; but after pumping for an hour, and not getting even a rolling suck,
the mate gave orders to sound ; when, to the dismay
of the crew, it was found that nine inches of water
still remained in the well. The men had been hard

at work all day; there was every sign of a heavy easterly gale; yet the dismal work of pumping had to go steadily on. At midnight the gale increased, and the watch was called out to close-reef the topsails. The owner would not have been pleased had he heard the language that was used by the men on the yard-arms. One speaker went so far as to express a wish that his employer was lashed under the cathead; and, since the cathead was never above water, the suggestion was received with much applause. The "Wansbeck" had sailed on the 8th of the month, and until the 11th the pumps were kept constantly going. The morning of the 12th broke with a wan glare in the sky, and a tremendous sea came away. The captain was obliged to veer the ship with her head to the north, and she went away fast before the gale under two close-reefed topsails. The men's hands were beginning to get badly damaged by the constant labour, but no rest was possible. On the 13th the wind rose to a hurricane; and masses of water were flung bodily down on the vessel, so that she was immersed most of the time and the sailors worked on up to their waists in pouring water. As one of the crew said, "things was no mistake dreadful." At the end of every watch the men who should have gone below were forced to take a two hours' spell at the pump; they then wrung their clothes, hung them up before the little fire in the forecastle, and turned in naked. Then, after a brief snatch of sleep, they jumped out, put on their steam-ing clothes, and went to the pumps once more. At 6 a.m. on the 14th the handspike was thumped on the deck, and a sailor said, "Turn out, boys; she's going down!" Worn out with want of rest, their hands and feet half flayed, the men staggered out and went desperately to work again. The brakes of the pumps hung far above their heads, and after toiling for three hours one of the standards broke and things looked hopeless. By six o'clock next day there were four and a half feet of water in the hold, and still the struggle was kept up with dogged resolution. At ten o'clock the water had risen to six feet, and all the time the hurricane blew with unabated force. The ship was plunging away northward, and not a sail could be seen on all the grey waste of the sea.

Now the crew went aft and told the captain that they could not keep the "Wansbeck" floating much longer; they thought the flag should be put in the main rigging, "union down." The captain said, "All right, my lads. There's but poor hopes for us, I know, whether we take to the boat or stick to the ship. Take your own way and do what you think is best. Our time will soon be over." So the flag was hoisted, and the men prepared for the end—without fear, for sheer physical misery had made them dull and silently reckless. The captain told a young hand to go into the forepeak and see if the water had reached far up: the same hand was ordered to clear away the longboat. Now the fore-trysail had come down on the boat; and when it was flung down the young seaman noticed that it seemed to be sucked down into a kind of eddy. There had been so many false alarms that the lad did not say anything until he had examined this new phenomenon carefully. Wading forward, he felt cautiously with his bare feet and found that his toes went into a

large hole.   He called out, " Here's the big leak; our
decks are stove in ! " and indeed it was this hole,
through which the constant burden of water on deck
had poured, that had caused the pumps to be mastered.

After some very hard work the leak was stopped,
and the men began to labour with new heart. The
courage of the men had revived, and they cheered each
other on.   For four hours the whole crew went at it
with a will; torn and bleeding hands were unheeded,
and the thought of death was put away.   All the same
the boat was kept ready for leaving the ship; but just
as the night came down and the white crests began to
lighten on the following seas, the pump sucked slightly,
and the crew knew that they might stand by the
vessel.   For six-and-twenty hours they had been on
deck without a spell; they had been working in an in-
cessant flood of water ; their sleeves had been doubled
up, and every man had ugly salt-water boils on his
arms.   The little cabin-boy had stuck gallantly to
work with the rest, but both his feet were frost-bitten,
and he could not stand alone.   A more deplorable
ordeal was never undergone by men, and nothing but
indomitable hardihood could have kept them up.   On
the 17th of the month they had got so far north that
there was scarcely any daylight in each twenty-four
hours.   At noon on that day the poor fellows saw a
thing which was not calculated to cheer them.   They
were looking gloomily out, when a little brig like their
own seemed to start up amid the driving haze.   She
laboured past them; and then they watched her stagger,
stop, and founder.   Next day they ran into a com-
parative calm; and when the " Wansbeck " reached

latitude 65 degrees north, the sea fell away, and the brig was safe. Then the men felt the misery of their sores; for after they slept for a while the act of unclosing the hands was terribly painful. The poor boy was very resigned and brave. He could not be helped in any way, and both his feet had to be cut off when the vessel reached Malmo.

A few days' fine weather enabled the crew to repair sails and broken gear; then the " Wansbeck " clawed her way down the Norwegian coast and got into the " Sleeve." What the men longed for most was tobacco; and when at the end of some days' sailing they sighted a Dutch galliot they boarded her, and the poor English scarecrows were helped liberally. That night was passed in smoking and a blessed forgetfulness of pain. The " Wansbeck " was given up at home, and some women had put on mourning before she was heard of. Nothing could have saved her had not the young seaman seen that ugly dangerous place where the falling yard had smashed the deck in ; and the owner had to thank the dogged hopeless bravery of his men for saving the brig even after the great leak was discovered. The " Wansbeck " is still running; but she has patent rigging and serviceable pumps, and probably her owner is not so much the object of unfriendly wishes.

THE men who go away in the great smacks and remain at sea for many weeks at a time are used to call themselves fishermen; but the long-shore fisher does not consider these smacksmen as being members of his profession at all. A person who leaves his own village, and never comes home in the morning like a decent citizen, is regarded with much condescension by the owner of a coble. The bolder voyager calls himself a fisher, but he is really only a kind of sailor; and as such he is a being to be patronized by the true craftsman. Right up the coast, from the Tyne to Berwick, little villages are planted at intervals of about four miles; and these villages are mostly inhabited by men who only use open boats. The ethnologists say that, as regards height, chest measurement, and strength, the population of this strip of coast shows the finest men in the world. The Cumberland dalesmen are often very tall; but in weight and girth of chest the mountaineers are not equal to the Northumbrian fishers. Dr. Brown has published some curious statistics bearing on this point; and he is of opinion that the flower of the English race may be found within a circle of two or three miles around the village of Boulmer. The villages are much alike in every respect. The early settlers seem to have looked for places where a range of low rocks lay like the string of a bow across the curve of a bay, or where a cove nestled under the southerly steep of a jutting point. The beaches shelve very gradually, and are never shingly; so that a special kind of boat gradually had to be contrived in order that the peculiar nature of the landing might be suited. The early fishermen saw that the boat must have a very light draught of water, and yet be sufficiently weatherly to face the open sea. Thus, after years of experiment, the " coble " was designed in its present form ; and these craft are as much the product of their special locality as are the men who man them. The coble has an exceedingly deep bow, which grips the water to a depth of some three feet, and which resembles in contour the breastbone of a grebe or northern diver. This great curve is rimmed with iron. But from the bend the lines slope upward, until at the stern the boat is quite flat-bottomed and only about three feet in depth. She is poised so that while her bow draws three feet of water her stern will float in one or two inches ; and she will come so near the shore that one can climb over her stern nearly dryshod. In smooth water she may be rowed about very easily and safely ; but it would be impossible to carry sail on a craft of which really only one-half of the keel is submerged: she would capsize instantly in a very light wind. This difficulty is cleverly met. As soon as the coble is put under sail her great rudder is fixed ; and this rudder, which is very broad, goes under water to a depth of three feet or so. When the wind is on the beam the rudder acts exactly like a centre-board : if it breaks, nothing can save the coble; but so long as it holds the vessel will lie well over and sail with amazing swiftness. Years upon years of apprenticeship are needed before a man can manage one of these crank boats; in fact, the fishermen's proverb says, "You must be born in a coble if you want to learn anything about her."

The race of men who work in the cobles have good chances of becoming skilful, for they begin very early. When the fisher-boy has passed the merest infancy his steps tend to the water-side as naturally as though he were a young sea-bird. He carries the water-bottles down to the boats in the afternoon, and sees his father and the other men hauling off out of the shallow cove. The evening comes down, and he watches the race northward until the last brown sail has passed around the point. In the morning he is ready for the boats as they come home, and he can distinguish each craft exactly, although an outsider would be able to see not a whit of difference. He sees the fish carted, and then goes home with the stolid heavy-footed men. All the morning, while the fishermen are sleeping, the fisher-lad is busy helping the women to bait lines or spread nets, according to the season. He goes in an amateur way to school, but he is the wildest and most gipsy-like of scholars. His thoughts have suffered a sea change, and he takes badly to books and slates. A studious fisherman is hardly to be found, and it is only within the last twenty years that the accomplishment of reading has become known in the smaller villages. Since the Government school system spread, many little places have been established; but what can a poor schoolmaster do with a pupil who is wanted nearly every morning to gather bait on the rocks, and who must see the trouting boats off on the summer afternoons ? The fisher-boy always goes bare-footed. Big sea-boots suit him when he grows up, but the shabby compromise of shoes or " bluchers " is totally unacceptable to him. When he goes to school he sometimes puts the hated footgear on ; but as soon as the prison-doors are passed he slings the boots round his neck and goes merrily home with his brown feet moving freely. He will charge through a clump of nettles quite indifferently; and this wondrous power strikes civilized children with awe. The fisher-boy's language is a strange mixture. No southerner can understand him; for, besides using old words, the fisher speaks with harsh gutturals that make a burring sound in his throat. He calls a wild cherry a " guigne;" he calls a swede turnip a " baygee," a gooseberry a " grozer," mud " clarts," a horse-collar a " brime." If he had to say " I fell head over heels," he would remark, " Aw cowped me creels." The stranger is puzzled by this surprising tongue, but the fisher is proud of it. No words can express his scorn for a boy who learns to talk " Massingem " (which is the fisher's word for English): he scouts that degenerate boy and refuses to consort with him. When the fisher-lad gets measured for his first oilskins he is very proud. To " get away Norrad " is the right of men ; and he feels himself manly as he sits amidships while the coble skims out into the bay. He is usually sent to the trouting first ; and then all night long he glides about on the dark bay and hears the sounds from the moor and the woods. It falls cold toward the dawn, and the boy grows hard and strong through his nightly ordeal. When his hands are properly hardened like his horny feet, he is allowed to row the coble with crossed oars; and then he becomes very useful, for the men are left free to haul nets and plash on the water to frighten the trout. When he reaches the age of sixteen, the fisher-lad clothes himself in thick pilot-cloth and wears a braided cap on Sundays. He pierces his ears too, and his thin golden rings give him a foreign look. The young fisher-folk are very shamefaced about sweet-hearting. A lad will tramp eight miles after dark to see his sweetheart; but he would be stupefied with shame if anyone saw him walking with her. The workman of the towns escorts his lover on Sunday afternoons, and is not ashamed; but the fisher-folk never walk openly in couples.

Courtship is a very unpoetic affair with them. No one ever heard a fisher use such a word as " love: " he would not consider himself a man if he once learned such a fragment of " Massingem." If by any chance the village grows crowded and some of the young men have to go southward to the seaports, then those who return may bring sailor-like ways with them; but the natives always remain hard and undemonstrative.

It is difficult to say when the fisher-lad is considered to have reached man's estate. A good deal depends on his physical development. The work to be done at sea is so very heavy that only a very powerful fellow can perform it. It sometimes happens that a very strong lad of eighteen can do a " man's turn; " but usually a fisherman must be thoroughly " set " before he is counted as one of the elect. He then begins to think of marriage, and his long Sunday evening journeys become frequent. He must marry a fisher-girl; for if he chooses a hind's daughter he is as badly off as a one-armed man. The work done by the fisher-women needs long and special training : the baiting of lines is a delicate and subtle operation, while the business of seeking bait is one which no country-woman ever learns properly. Moreover, a country girl who has been used to wearing long dresses and shoes can never take kindly to bare feet and brief petticoats : the cold and exposure are too much for her. A fisherman who marries a girl from inland is considered to have wrecked his chances in life, and the gossips bewail his fate. He is shut off from social intercourse ; for his wife, even though she may have lived within two miles of the sea, cannot meet the clannish fishers on equal terms. If, however, the fisherman marries according to natural law, he and his wife begin their partnership without any of the frivolities of wedding trips and such like. The girl settles down quickly ; and in a week she is baiting lines in the stone-floored kitchen, or tramping inland with her great fish basket slung round her forehead. She bows her strong figure under her burden, and the great pad which prevents the rope from cutting her brow looks like a strange head-dress. Her husband is too secretive to exhibit any pride, but he is satisfied with his helpmate.

The fisherman has no amusements. In the afternoons, when his sleep is over, he walks up and down in the Row and gazes around ; but he rarely laughs, and few things interest him unless he is religious. Fishermen seldom gossip like rustics. Sometimes they have a queer dry humour which comes out in short phrases, but they never carry on sustained conversation. The faculty of expression is granted them in very sparing degree. The fisherman's courage is perfect, yet he cannot speak of his own actions. He will do the most brave things in a stolid, unconscious way; but he could not frame a hundred consecutive words to tell anyone what he had done. He never shows any emotion excepting when under the influence of religious excitement. The melancholy of the sea seems to have entered his nature, and his chief efforts aim at self-restraint. When the little Methodist chapel resounds with the noise of appreciative groanings and sighing, it is very rarely that anything like gesticulation or vivid facial change is seen. Deep-chested men utter sonorous ejaculations and the women sigh, but there is no shuffling of feet and no movement. As a class, the fishers have grown to be more religious than almost any other body of men, and they like powerful excitement; but they are always severely decorous. In his behaviour toward his social superiors the fisherman is rugged—perhaps morbidly rugged—but his brusque familiarity is not offensive. To touch his cap would be impossible to him, but his direct salute is neither self-assertive nor impolite. The fisherman toils on till the time comes for him to stay ashore always. His life is a very risky one, and the history of every village is largely made up of stories about drowned men, for the coast is an ugly place, and the utmost skill and daring can hardly carry a man through a lifetime without accident. If the accident is fatal, there is an end of all : the bruised bodies are washed up ; the women wring their hands, and the old men walk about silently. But if things go well, then the fisherman's old age is comfortable enough. The women look after him kindly, and on sunny mornings he enjoys himself very well as he nurses the children on the bench facing the sea.

THE "Halicore" ran into harbour one October morning and took up her berth at the quay. The brig had come from a nine months' voyage and the men were regarded as heroes when they came ashore, for most of our vessels were merely coasters. When all was made snug on board, the sailors went to their homes and received the admiring homage of the neighbours. One young man whose parents lived in a cottage away to the north was very keen to get home. He had a weary stretch of moorland to pass, and the evening was wild, with only fitful gleams of moonlight to brighten the dark, but the young sailor would not stay. He knew the old people would be sitting by the fireside till half-past ten or eleven, and it delighted him to think how they would start with joy when he rattled the latch on the door. An innkeeper warned him about the state of the roads, but the sailor was a light-hearted fellow, and paid no heed to the talk about "muggers," or gipsies. He had been very careful during the voyage, so that his leather belt under his waistcoat was well filled with sovereigns and silver. Of course he knew that the "muggers," (or travelling potters), were sometimes nasty customers to meet on a dark night, but he reckoned that he could hold his own anywhere. Jack was well-built, and very swift of foot, and he strode fast over the dark and misty moor. The furze bushes roared as the wind went through, and the heather made a mysterious whispering, but Jack did not mind the noises that affect the nerves of cultured persons. A poacher bade him a kindly good-night, and added, "Mind there'll be some queer fellows along by the Dead Man's Trail," but Jack did not turn back, although he felt the poacher's warning a little. Rabbits scampered past him, and an owl beat steadily over the heather like a well-trained setter. When the dark grew thicker the wail of the curlews as they called from overhead was strange. The howl of a fox, that weirdest of all sounds, came sharply from among the brown brackens, but Jack was not impressed : he was home again, and the piercing cry of the fox was only a pleasant reminder of good fortune.

Presently three men stopped the traveller, and asked the road to the port from which he had just come. One of them struck a match and managed to throw a gleam on Jack's face before the wind put the flame out. By the same light, the sailor saw that the three men were muggers, and that they were not pleasant-looking people. He disengaged himself and walked swiftly north for about thirty yards. A thud of feet made him turn, and from one brief glance he knew that the men were making a rush for him. He gathered his energies instantly, and struck off at his best speed. He was an excellent runner and a good jumper, so that he gradually drew away from his pursuers until he lost the sound of their feet; but he knew that they were doggedly following, and that his only chance was to reach the ferry, and get the ferryman to help him. Now this same ferry plied across a swift stream that ran into the sea about two and a half miles north of the place where he met the men. The current was so very strong that no boatman could possibly row from bank to bank: the boat would have been swept out to sea. So a strong chain had been run across the river, and the boat was fastened to a ring which ran along this chain. The ferryman simply stood in the bow of the wherry and hauled her across by main force, passing the ring along as he went. Every night the chain was lowered into the water, and the man left his little boat, and went westward to his proper home. It should be said that the chain could be wound from either bank, for a winch was placed at each side.

Jack was badly out of breath when he reached the ferry, and he felt minded to lie down, but there was no time for resting. He ran to the water's edge, and found the man and boat gone, the hut dark, and the chain lowered. The stream poured past like a millrace, and he looked hopelessly on the swift water. At first he thought of turning to take his fate. He had his clasp knife and he could die fighting if they really meant to murder him. Then he thought of his money and the good it would do at home, and he determined to try once more. He ran to the winch and bent himself at it; the chain came up and gradually tightened until he saw dimly that the long arc was quite clear of the water. Just as he had clenched the winch the foremost of the footpads came down the hill and shouted as he saw the sailor. Jack got underneath the chain, took firm hold with his hands and twisted his legs round as though he were climbing a back-stay ; then he began to haul himself across. Before he had gone forty yards he felt that there was someone else clambering along that awkward support, but he knew that forty yards more would make him safe. He was nearly smothered at the place where the chain dipped lowest, for the water was coming in freshets; but he hung on, and landed panting and with grazed limbs on the north bank. By the shaking of the chain he knew that the mugger was coming along, and he decided in a flash to take strong measures. There was a good surplus to run out, so he set the winch free. He heard one loud cry, and then there was silence. He had drowned the footpad. The best swimmer on the coast could not have got to the shore in that place.

Jack's nerve was completely gone, and he could hardly raise a trot. He used to laugh much about the terrors that he suffered during the remainder of his journey. First of all he trod on a young rabbit, and the shrill squeak that came sent his heart to his mouth; then, just as he neared his home, the shepherd's donkey took the fancy to bray with vigour, and Jack thought for one moment that another enemy was upon him. Presently he saw the light in his own window, and he knew that he was in honest regions once more. The old people were much amazed when their son came in, bareheaded, wet, and covered with red rust from the friendly chain, but they were glad to see him in any plight. The moor is in much better order now-a-days, for the muggers are all driven away north to Yetholm and Wooler. A stately policeman traverses

K

the bank once every night, and no one is ever molested. The first policeman was stabbed from behind, and flung over the cliff, but there has been no mischief since that time, and the district is very quiet indeed.

HOB'S TOMMY.

THE moor was blazing in the sun. Bright gorse flamed above the pale green grass, and little pools flashed white rays up to the sky. Hob's Tommy stepped out of doors, and took a long look round. He was not impressed by the riot of colour that spread around him; he looked over the pulsing floor of the sea, and thought, "It will be a fine night for the trouting."

Tommy was a large man, who seemed to shake the ground as he trod. His face was devoid of speculation, and his dull blue eyes looked from under heavy and unamiable brows. His hair was matted, and his mode of dressing his big limbs showed that he was careless of opinion. He was called Hob's Tommy because the villagers had a fancy for regarding sons as the personal property of the father, and thus a man called Thomas, who happened to be the son of a man called John, never received his surname during his whole life, excepting on the occasions of his baptism and marriage. He was known as Jack's Tom. If he, in his turn, happened to have a son whom he chose to name Henry, the youth was known as Jack's Tom's Harry. Our friend Tommy's father had been called Hob, and hence the name of the ill-tempered lout who was gazing on the unsullied sea. Tommy watched the green water breaking over the brown sand, and far out at sea he saw the thick haze still brooding low. He knew the evening would be fine, and he knew that he would have a good basket for next day's market. He put his hands in his pockets, and strolled away from the unsavoury neighbourhood of the Fishers' Row on to the glistening moor. His eyes were fixed on the ground, and into his mind entered no thought saving calculations about money and drink. Any stranger who had met him walking over the thyme, with his fierce face bent downward, would have gained a bad notion of the local population. A sudden jangle of bells filled the air, and the ringers went to work gaily. Quaint farmers went along dressed in creased suits of clothing; quiet country women nodded as they passed, but Tommy heeded none of his neighbours. He was a brutal man, whose presence seemed an insult to the holy morning. He walked mechanically on over the moor, and let the sound of church bells die away in his ear. Presently he came to a beautiful slope, which was starred with pink geraniums. The sun shone warmly upon it, and a lark flashed from amid the flowers with a sound of joy, and carried his rejoicing up into the sky. Tommy thought, "This is a nice warm place to lie down on. I'll light my pipe." And he stretched himself amid the tender flowers. The glow and the colour of the life around him, and the sparkle of the sea, seemed at last to make some dim suggestion to his mind. He said, half aloud, "Wonder what I'm here for.

I don't know. I only wish it was seven o'clock and the sun droppin';—he was a lazy man that invented Sunday;—another day I'll away to the fishin' i' the mornin', and the folks can say just what they like. I'm not goin' to waste my time and my baccy lyin' on sandhills." So he smoked on until the sun reached its greatest height, and the afternoon shadows lay like dark pansies in the hollows.

Now it happened that in the neighbouring village it was usual to hold an afternoon service and an evening service in the Wesleyan chapel. The services followed close on each other, and there was great competition among the villagers as to who should give the preacher his tea in the interval. Tommy presently found himself looking sleepily at a man who was bent over the moor to attend the chapel. If you had met the new-comer, you would have been compelled to look back at him. He was tall and spare. His shoulders were very broad, and he walked with a kind of military tread. His face was good to see; the calm and joy of the bright day seemed to have entered his soul, and his eyes looked as though he were thinking of things too deep for words. His mouth was sternly closed, and yet despite its tension the delicate lines at the corners seemed to speak of humour and tenderness. His hat was thrown back a little, and showed a large forehead marked by slight lines, which spoke not so much of temper as of placid musing. He was murmuring to himself as he walked, and he seemed to be in communion with a multitude of exquisite thoughts. When he reached the bank where the geraniums grew, his placidity quickened into alertness as he saw the figure of Tom stretched upon the grass. He stepped up to the lounger and said, in a low cheery tone—

"Well, Thomas, my man, and what takes you out at this time of day? I suppose you are having a bit of a rest after yesterday?"

Thomas answered in the following terms :—

"I don't know what business it is of yours what I am doing. If you want to know what I am here for, I'll tell you. I am thinking how I can cheat the Conservancy men to-night. I wish you good-day."

The tall man was not by any means surprised by the uncourteous answer. He was used to the homely insolence of the fishermen. So he said—

"Well, Thomas, I was young myself once, and I liked to lounge on the Sunday as well as anybody; but it's God's Sabbath, and after all, you know, my lad, you are not a pig, and I think you might be doing ever so much better things than lying here. I am not a bit of a saint, and I am not going to bother you about religion, but it struck me, as I came across the moor, that I was happy, and you are not. Now I'll tell you what I am going to do, Thomas—you won't throw me over the rock-edge, because I am rather an awkward hand at that sort of thing. I am going to sit down and have a pipe beside you. Will you give me a light?"

Tommy could not condescend to a grin, but he observed—

"Sit down and smoke as many pipes as you like, so long as you leave me alone, Mr. Musgrave."

Musgrave knew his man, and answered smilingly—

"But I am not going to sit down to smoke and keep quiet. I want to have a bit of talk to you; and as soon as I am done I am going to take you with me. What do you think of that, Thomas?" And thereupon the old man lighted his pipe, and sat smiling for a little and moving his long fingers daintily. When the two queer companions had taken puff by puff together for some time, Musgrave said—

"Thomas, my lad, you are very unhappy. I am happy, and I think a man has no more right to keep happiness to himself than he has to keep money to himself. I am going to share with you. Now, I'm an old fellow that's got near done with the world, and you are a slashing young chap, and the girls look after you. But still, though I am parting with the world, and you have got a long time to stay in it, I am better off than you. The sight of these flowers makes me joyful, but it only seems to make you dour. Now, shall I tell you how it is that I am so happy?"

"I don't want to be happy. What's that got to do with the thing? If you tell me that there's fifty sovereigns buried at the bottom of Lyne Hill there, I'll go and try to dig the hill away and get at them, because the trouble's worth taking; but I don't see the fun of seeking for what you call happiness."

"Well, then, Thomas, how much do you expect to make by trouting to-night?"

"Well, if there's any luck, Jem and me will divide fifteen shillings between us."

"Very good; then I'll give you seven-and-six-pence now. Here are your three half-crowns. Will you come with me?"

The sulky giant smiled sourly and said, "I don't see why I should not.   Where are you for?"

"Well, I am going to preach at the chapel, Thomas, and I would like you to hear me and walk home with me, and I think that when I have landed you at your house that you won't be sorry for missing the trouting."

Tommy rose heavily up, shook the fragments of dry grass from his patched garments, and signified that he was ready.   Musgrave took his arm, and at once assumed an attitude of companionship and equality. He talked with this churl about all manner of trivialities, flattered him, appealed to his sense of shrewdness, made little jokes suitable to his wit, and finally succeeded in making him feel himself to be rather a clever and entertaining person.   The afternoon sun sloped lower and lower as the two strolled over the moor.   Musgrave's thoughts were high, although his words ran upon childish things.   He had no particular artistic sense, but the joy of colour, the blaze of the sky, the warm and exhilarating air, made him feel as though he must utter praises.   After passing some miles of strange moorland, covered with the blaze of gorse, and the multitudinous flash of marshy pools, the two arrived at a curious square building, which stood a little outside the fishing village.

Musgrave said, "Now, Thomas, come in, and I'll find you a pew," and the two entered a low room. The congregation was already collected.   There were fierce faces, bronzed by wind and sun.   There were quiet faces that bore the marks of thought and the memories of toil.   The men were all rudely dressed,

and the women wore the primitive clothing which for
three hundred years past has served for the simple
tastes of the villagers. After a pause of a few minutes,
Walter Musgrave's tall figure loomed in the shadowy
corner where the pulpit stood. A simple hymn was
dictated and sung in strong nasal tones. The old
man who led the singing prided himself upon the
volume of sound which he could at any instant propel
through his nose. Strangers were sometimes a little
disconcerted by this feat, for it seemed as if some
wholly new description of trumpet had been suddenly
invented. This man of the trumpet voice was wont
to close his eyes and turn his face towards the ceiling.
When once the preliminary blast had been blown from
his nostrils, no power on earth could stay the flood of
song. He became oblivious of time and space and the
congregation. Considerations as to harmony did not
enter into his scheme of the universe. If he got
flagrantly wrong, he simply coughed and took up the
thread of the musical narrative where he left off.
The congregation had a great notion of his powers.
They considered that the terrific drone with which he
opened a hymn could not be equalled in any church or
in any chapel for twenty miles round.

Musgrave suffered a good deal under the storm of
harmony, but he always bore it bravely, and, when
possible, lent the aid of his own high, sweet tenor, to
the nasal clamour. After the hymn came a short
prayer, delivered as though the speaker really believed
that his God was at hand, and would instantly listen to
any petition humbly proffered by frail creatures. At
the end of a short pause, Walter Musgrave stood up to

speak. He broadened his chest and straightened himself, unconsciously hinting at his physical power. He then read his text in a low voice: " *Why is life given to a man whose way is hid, and whom God hath hedged in?* " Musgrave was an uneducated man, with strong logical instincts. Perhaps, had he been educated thoroughly, the poetic vein, which gave the chief charm to his mind and conversation, would have been destroyed. As it was, he invariably confined himself to logic so long as his emotions remained untouched; but there were moments when his blood seemed to catch fire, and he broke away from the calm reasoning which serves for placid men. He then spoke with poetry, and with an accent which affected the nerves of all who heard him. On this afternoon he began with a little sketch of the history of Job, and he then detailed his notion that the Arab, who wrote the most wonderful book in the world, was really the type of the modern man, and lived hundreds of generations before his time. He pointed out that all around us in Britain were men of deep thoughts, and wise thoughts, who had grown discontented with the world, and had set up their own intelligence in an endeavour to grasp the purpose of an intelligence infinitely higher. The existence of evil, the existence of pain, the existence of all the things that make men's pilgrimage, from dark to dark, mysterious and awful, can never be probed to any purpose by one creature created by the great Power who also created the mystery of pain and the problem of evil. Dwelling in the desert, and seeing day by day the movements of the world, and the

strange progress of the stars, Job had grown to
cherish the pride of intellect. So long as his pros-
perity was unbroken, he was contented, and busied
himself day after day in relieving the wants of the
poor and in succouring the oppressed. But when the
blast of affliction blew upon him, his kindly disposition
forsook him for a little, and he only thought of his own
bitterness ; he only thought of the puzzles that have
faced every man who has a heart to feel since first our
race appeared in this wondrous place. Musgrave
thought that every man who has faith, every man
whose heart has been torn by the wrenches of chance,
must sympathize with the yearning of Job ; but at
the last every man, like Job, comes to see that there
are things beyond our minds. Each of us learns that
there are things before which our intelligence must be
abashed, and that the only safe rule of life is to fall
into the attitude of trust, and question no more. He
felt it necessary to touch his homely hearers, and he
said : " Only last week the wind woke from the sky,
and the storm swept over the moor, and swept over
this little place where two or three are now gathered
together to worship. Many of our friends put forth
in the morning in the joy of strength, in the pride
of manhood, and no one of them fancied the sea
that now fawns upon the shore would wake up into
fury, and would dash its claws into cliff and sand,
and rend the works of man into nothingness. We
stood together on these cliffs—wives whose husbands
were wrestling with the storm, mothers who were
yearning for the sons they had borne. We saw
the boats fight nearer and nearer through the mad

spray and the tearing blasts. One after another we saw them crushed and sunken by the hand of the wind. Many of us went to our homes with bitterness at heart. We could not tell why those innocent men should have been snatched out of life; we could not tell why the innocent sufferers who remain should bear their sorrow through all the years until the release of death comes. Our thoughts were the thoughts that Job cherished in the black depths of his agony. But let me counsel you; let me ask you to remember that although death is here and pain is here—although every moment of our lives brings some new mystery —yet in the end there shall be peace. Our little sufferings count as nothing in the sum of the universe. The ills that we cry out against are only but as the troubles of children, and over all watches the Father who cared for Job in the desert, and who took to His own breast the souls of those who went down in the storm that crushed so many hopes of so many men and women in this our little village. I ask you only to trust. I give you no arguments. I only beg you to feel. Crush your questionings. Force yourself to believe in your own insignificance; force yourself to think that suffering has a wise end, and that even our pains, which are so great to us, are part of the scheme of a Master who is moulding the universe to His own plans. When once you have attained this central attitude of calm and trust, then for the rest of your life you will know nothing but joy. The thought of death will be no more like to the horror of a nightmare, but you will meet the great change even as you meet the deep black sleep

of tired men. You will know, while thought remains, that you have not lived in vain, and you have
not died in vain, for somewhere in God's providence
there shall be rest for you, and immortal peace."

The thin frame of the speaker quivered as he
spoke, and his long fingers writhed with a motion
that gave emphasis to his ringing tones. Hob's
Tommy had never heard anything like this before.
He sat stupefied, and felt as though some music not
heard of hitherto were playing and giving him gladness. The congregation broke up, and old William
Dent said to one of his cronies, " Watty was grand
this afternoon. Ay, they may talk about the fine
preachers with the Greek and the Latin, but I want
to hear a man like that." Musgrave and Hob's
Tommy walked back over the moor in the twilight
after the second service, and the giant spoke not a
word all the way until they reached the bridge that
crossed the little river. The dying twilight made the
sluggish water like silver, and the trees were just
beginning to moan with the evening wind. Tommy
stood in the middle of the bridge, and looked—looked
into the dark depths of the water, and then let his eye
trace the silver path of the river where it vanished
in the soft purple tints of the wood. He said, "If I was
to drop over here now, Mr. Musgrave, do you think
God would take me ?" And Musgrave said—

" Don't talk nonsense, Thomas; come along with
me. When God wants to take you, He will take you ;
but you must not be trying to put your opinions in place
of God's. Turn back, my man, and look at the Point
there where the Cobbler's Stone stands. Now forget

that you are looking at the calm stream, and think what you would feel like one dark night, with a northerly gale, if you had to fight your way round the Cobbler, and expected the sea to double over your boat every minute. You are not in danger now, and your business is to worship. Try to think, my lad, what you would feel if you expected that every sea would be the last one. Now come away, and talk no more nonsense to-night."

So Hob's Tommy did not go trouting on that Sunday evening.

The next day, when he woke up, he had a sense of strangeness, and it suddenly flashed upon him that he ought to pray. He did not exactly know how to begin, but he managed to produce a curious imitation of the prayer he had heard Musgrave deliver the day before. He then put on his sea-boots and sou'-wester, and strolled into the kitchen. When his mother heard his foot in the passage, she trembled a little, because Tom was not over civil as a rule. To her utter astonishment, the ruffian whom she loved said, "Good morning, mother. Is the coffee ready?" He then stepped up to her, and placed his arm round her shoulders. He had never kissed anybody in his life; so that form of endearment did not occur to him; but he bent his bearded face, and laid his cheek clumsily against his mother's. The draggled woman was so startled that she was unable to form any idea as to the possible cause of this transformation. She only said, "Sit down, my bonny man, and your bacon will be ready for you in two minutes. I have never seen you look so well in my life. Will I be sending to the town for some bottled beer for you by the time you get back ? "

" No, mother; I am going to try and do without the drink for a bit. I hit you last Saturday night, didn't I ? "

" Well, don't speak about that, my bonny man."

" Show us the mark, mother."

She bared her arm to the shoulder, and there, sure enough, was a black bruise.

He ate his breakfast and went out, leaving his mother in a condition of exaltation which she had not known for many years. All the day, while the lines were over the side, Tommy sat with his face in his hands. His two mates joked with him, swore at him, tried all kinds of clumsy inducements to make him revert to his ordinary saturnine and entertaining mode of conversation; but he would not be tempted from his silence. Towards evening a chill blast struck off from the shore, and Mary's Jem, who was Tommy's mate, said—

" My man, we'll have the white horses in half a minute ! "

A short, jumping sea sprang up as if by magic; the men hauled in their lines, took three reefs in the coble's main-sail before hoisting, and then laid the boat's head for the land. Minute by minute the blast grew heavier; quick gusts shook the bents on the sandy hills, and screamed away over the moaning floor of the sea. The boat had to beat very near the wind, and, as she ducked and plunged to the short rollers, clouds of spray came aboard, varied by plunges of green water. Sailing within three and a half points of the wind, and with her three reefs in the lug, she made at least four knots, and the water roared under her rudder. Jemmy lit his pipe, and said—

"We'll have to run north, my man."

Tommy said, energetically,—

"No, I'll not. The old woman is going to make my supper for me, and I'll not disappoint her, if I'm drowned in trying."

So the boat raced towards the bay, bows under. Nearing the Carr, where a narrow passage opens into smooth water, a strong back-wash came from the jagged rocks. One curling black sea came foaming back, and met the green sea that was plunging on to the reef. A mountain of water rose and fell with a heavy crash over the sail, and the boat turned slowly over. All three men were encumbered with their heavy sea-boots, but they managed to struggle out and fasten themselves on to the high keel. Four or five seas came in quick succession; the boat reached shallow water; the mast snapped with a loud crash, and within a few seconds Tommy said—

"Jump now, men, for it."

Up to their waists in water, the men clambered on to the sand and looked round, only to see the wreck of their coble beating herself to pieces with heavy lunges twenty yards from the shore.

Tommy spat the salt water out of his mouth, and fell upon his knees. He then walked up to the village, changed his clothes, behaved with elephantine tenderness to his mother, and walked out in the darkness to see his friend, the gardener. He sat on the settle in the low kitchen, and smoked solemnly without speaking. The next night he appeared at the same hour, and spent his evening in the same composed manner. For three weeks he never missed a night, and the gardener's family were puzzled to an extraordinary degree by the sombre expression of his face, and by his abstinence from the rude remarks which were wont to characterize his conversation concerning his friends and neighbours. Mrs. Wray, the gardener's wife, said one evening, "I wonder what the lout comes doddering about here for. He sits as if some of the lads had cutten his tongue out." The very next night Tommy solved her obstinate questionings. He said, "Mary, my hinny, I have found God;" and the next afternoon Walter Musgrave was astonished and pleased to see the fierce face of Tommy glaring from the seat opposite the pulpit. This dumb man had no means of expressing the feelings that were taking possession of him. He only knew that he felt kindly towards all living things, and, above all, he felt as though he must manifest a feeling akin to worship when he was in the gentle presence of Musgrave.

Year after year, until his mother died, he never failed in his kindness towards her, and the old dame was wont to express a kind of comic surprise at the womanish demeanour of her son. He caught fish for his living, but a cramped piece of reasoning forced him to the conclusion that it would be wrong for him to shoot any more birds. He said, "The birds was made by God, and God's been good to me, and I am not going to hurt them." Sunday after Sunday in all weathers he strode off to the moor. Wayfarers would meet him at night when the wind was hurling down from the Cheviots and bringing clouds of snow. He had but one salutation for all who met him : "Good night, my man; God bless you till the mornin'."

Sometimes, when the paths were so foul that nothing but wading would take a man over the moor, Tommy was greatly puzzled about finding his way, and one night he and Musgrave walked unsuspectingly over a low cliff, and fell softly upon a great ridge of sand. But these little misadventures did not by any means daunt Tommy. His new religion was that he must be at chapel twice every Sunday, and at prayer-meetings as often through the week as Musgrave chose to take him. To this he held. The Squire's pheasants suffered no longer, and Tommy's big lurcher displayed a tendency towards virtue which earned him the admiration of all the gamekeepers on the estate. Efforts were made to get the big man to pray at the ordinary love-feasts that were held in connection with the chapel, but he always said, "No; my Father and me has all our conversations to ourselves. It is not as if God didn't know; but I don't think a blackguard like me should address Him face to face after the life I have led."

The years went by, and Tommy's shaggy beard showed signs of grizzling. His huge limbs were more deliberate in their movement, and his low forehead had somehow or other acquired a certain spiritual aspect. He wrought at his trade, saved money, and spent some in decorating his mother's grave. One night, when he was smoking his pipe with Musgrave, he said—

"Christ died for all the lot of us, didn't He? That was a rare thing to do. Now, suppose He says, when I meet Him, ' What are you doing here? You have done nothing but go to chapel.' Now, Mr. Musgrave, will you tell me this : what should I say in a case of that sort?"

Old Musgrave wrinkled his wise brows and replied, "Thomas, my man, He knows your heart. I suppose you think you ought to save life, or something of that kind, don't you?"

" Yes, sir, that's just what I do think," said Thomas.

" Well, believe me, your chance will come. Now let's light up our pipes, and walk over the moor home, Thomas, and puzzle yourself no more about, these things."

A bad winter came, and the thundering seas broke so continually over the rocks that it was impossible for the men to get bait on their own rocks. All day long the loungers walked the cliff edge, and watched the columns of spray hissing up from the black rocks. Day after day the clouds seemed to mix themselves with the sea as they laid their grey shoulders to the water. Money became scarce in the village, and the men who had savings had to help those who were poorer. When things got almost too bad for bearing, Billy Armstrong said to one of his friends—

" Look here, you and me and Hob's Tommy will run round to the Tyne, and get some mussels, or else the whole place will be starved when the fine weather comes."

A big coble was got out, and ran down to the Tyne with a northerly wind through the shrewd and vicious

sea. The men got the cargo of mussels, and at four
in the afternoon prepared to beat their way northward.
It was then blowing half a gale, but the wind had
shifted round from the shore, so that very little tacking
was required. As the shades fell lower and lower, the
wind rose higher and higher. The blasts galloped
down through the hollows, and struck the brown sail
of the coble like the sound of musketry. The boat
lay hard over, and the water leaped in spurts over
her lee gunwale. They reached the point where the
Cobbler's Stone stood. Tommy was in a strange
state of exaltation. He pointed to the misty shore,
then to the black stone round which the water was
seething. He said quietly, "Yonder, my lads!"

They rounded the point, and put the boat's head
nearer to windward. A harsh ripping sound was heard
under the bottom. She lay hard over until a blast
came and tore her clear. Billy Armstrong said—

"You have taken her in a bit too near, my son.
The bilge chocks is both pulled off; look you, they're
gone away astern." And, sure enough, two long planks
drifted away behind the boat. They had been torn off
by the force with which she rushed upon the outlying
rock. Tommy said, "Let's have another reef in,
mates." But before the sail could be half lowered, a
storming gust swept out of the bay, and struck the
boat with a roar. The long rudder smashed; a green
sea doubled up behind her, and she turned over exactly
as the coble had done when Tommy first prayed.

In the wild waves it was hard for the men to get
hold. The bilge chocks were gone, and thus all
chance of a hand grip was lost. Half-way down the

square stern of the boat a hole had been bored, through which a rope had been passed and knotted at both ends. This rope served the men in hauling the boat down to the sea. Only one could hold on to this short scrap, and Tommy, who was the first to think of it, seized it, and held on with the strength of his despair. The boat lunged and struck the faces of the two men who were holding on to her sides. Billy Armstrong was bleeding from the mouth, and his front teeth were gone—dashed out by one stroke which had met him as he tried to climb and catch hold of the deep iron keel in the fore part of the coble. The other man said suddenly, " I have got a broken arm, Tommy." A few minutes went by, during which the men dared not speak—only Tommy was perfectly safe. The others were slipping and writhing in their efforts to hang on to the smooth planks. The man with the broken arm had the nails of his sound hand torn, and the blood streamed down as he clutched again and again at the slippery seams. At last he said, "I cannot do it any longer. Tell Mary the money is under the bed at the right-hand side next the wall, and ask my grandfather to take little Adam for me and keep him." A thought came into Hob's Tommy's mind. He cried out, " Don't let yourself go down. Edge yourself round here to the stern, and you shall have this rope." The maimed man came slowly round, and took the rope as Tommy let go. For a single minute the bruised giant rested his hands on the lunging stern of the little vessel. He did not look up, and his face had no devotional aspect, but the two men who were saved remembered his words to the end of their lives. He said, "O Lord Jesus, I am even with you now. I am going to die." The stern of the boat flew up into the air as a short sea hit her, and Hob's Tommy lost his grip. He lay back quietly on the water, and the men said that he even smiled. Presently the foam covered him over.

THE FAILURE.

TO the southward of the Chibburn Stream a flat
space, covered with rushes and grey grass,
stretches away towards the Border. On the seaward
side it is walled in by low hills, whilst on the land-
ward side a sudden rise of the ground forms another
boundary which makes the waste resemble the bed of
an ancient river. It was a favourite place with me in
the summer time, because the brackens grow here
and there, and to one who wants perfect seclusion
nothing can be more delightful than to creep under
the green shade and listen, hour after hour, to the
wind flying over. I had wanted to spend the whole
morning in this lazy way, so I put my Keats in my
pocket and walked along the sand until the time
came for me to climb the seaward barrier. I often
noticed a deserted cottage which stood at the northerly
end of the great waste, and which was sometimes used
in winter by the rabbit-catchers who had to remain
by their traps all night. Twice or thrice I had peeped
through the open door and seen the blackened hearth-
stone, but I had never gone inside. The remains of
a turf wall surrounded the cottage, but the low garden
that this wall enclosed was overrun with ragwort and
nettles and hemlock. My terrier was fond of investi-

gating the garden, because among the thick undergrowth he invariably found either rabbits or water-rats, or a stoat. On this bright morning I was much surprised to find the whole of the enclosure cleared. Outside of the boundary was a great heap of ashes, from which clouds of dust drifted hither and thither. A light smoke arose from the chimney, and as my dog and I approached, a heavy bark came from a mastiff that was chained inside the low wicket. A sudden sense of companionship almost frightened me. It seemed as though the brownie had come from his clump of rushes to set things in order. A chair stood in the centre of a patch of grass that crowned a little hillock near the cottage, and while I waited and wondered a bowed figure stole forth and walked slowly towards the chair. The man did not appear to notice me, but sat down and picked up a book which had lain on the grass. He then took off his hat, drew a deep breath, and I caught sight of his face. His grizzled hair hung over a careworn forehead. The eyes were sunken under deep and wrinkled brows, and the lips were drawn. I felt like an interloper, and determined to rid myself of all unpleasant feeling by stepping forward and speaking at once to the stranger. I could not think of anything better to say than " Good morning, sir. We have another fine day, have we not ? " The man looked up, and his tired eyes brightened with a kind smile. I took to him from that first glance. We had a little commonplace chat, and then I said, " I see you are a reader."

My new friend answered, " Oh, yes, I find books serve well to prevent anyone from thinking."

"But do you never think, then ?"

"Never, when I can help it; I take reading as an opiate. I press other men's thoughts down upon my own till mine cannot rise."

The queer smile with which the speaker delivered his paradox made me curious, and I determined to draw him further into conversation.

I continued, "May I ask what book you are using just now to batten down your own thoughts ?"

He showed me the "Purgatory," and I saw that he was reading the Italian. Here was a discovery! In the village I had been regarded as a remarkable being because I could read the Bible at six years old. The only persons who were reputed to possess learning of any sort were the Squire, the Rector, two local preachers, and myself. And now, suddenly, there had descended among us a scholar who positively read Dante for pleasure !

I continued the talk. "You will not think me rude if I ask why you should choose that book."

"I am afraid I must be more confidential than is seemly if I answer your question. Promise not to think me a babbler, and I will tell you. Dante is the poet for failures. I happen to be a failure, and as my life is broken I go to him for consolation."

This was a new vision of life to me, for generally our village talk was of crops, and the Squire's latest eccentricities.

When we had gossiped for a while about poetry and books in general, and when I had found that my acquaintance was far my superior in every possible respect, I prepared to move. He stopped me by saying " May I ask you, in turn, what book you are carrying ? "

" I read Keats. He is my Sunday luxury. I do not read him on the week-days for fear I should get him by heart, and every Sunday I start as though I were dipping into a new book."

" Ah ! then you still care for beauty. I used to feel positive physical luxury years agone while I read Keats, but now it seems as if the thought of beauty came between me and the grave. I am, like all the failures, a student of deformity. Strong men love beauty, futile men care only for ugliness. I am one of the futile sort, and so I care most for terror and darkness. Come inside, and perhaps I shall not talk quite so madly then."

The mastiff civilly let us pass, and I went into the low room of the cottage. One side was entirely taken up with books, and amongst the books were five editions of Dante. The fire blazed on the clean hearth,.and everything looked neat and well-kept. A narrow trestle bed stood in the corner, and a table and chair completed the furniture of the room.

I said, " You will find it horrible here when the winter comes on. The wind comes down from Chibburn Hollow, and when I was a boy I used to like to sit on the leeward side of the hills only to hear it scream."

" The wind will serve me for company."

I began to doubt my companion's sanity a little, and I said, " I am afraid talking has disturbed you. I must say good-bye."

I did not read that day, and the strange face with

its bitter mouth and keen eyes was in my memory for a week after. I set myself to inquire how this man, who could talk with such evident intelligence, came to have chosen the moor for an abiding-place, and it happened that by chance I learned his whole history.

I was walking across the moor with my friend the district local preacher, when a sudden whim prompted me to ask him to meet the strange creature whom I had seen. We went to the cottage, and were received by the deep baying of the dog. The stooping figure came out into the sunlight, and my friend the preacher said, "Bless my soul! Henry Desborough! What in the name of mercy has brought you here?"

Not a sign of emotion crossed the face of the Failure.

He said, "You ought to know, Musgrave. I was always a creature of whims."

"That is exactly what I do not know," said Musgrave.

"You are thinking of the times before I was twenty-five. Several centuries have passed over me since then."

Musgrave seemed unable to carry on the talk. He only said, "I take it very unkindly that you did not let me know you were here. I will come back and see you alone the next time. You have given me a sad heart for this day."

I knew now that there was a history in the case, and I learned it all from the man most concerned.

A long time ago a concert had been given in a small town somewhere down the coast. An imposing musician had been brought from London especially to train the choir, and the rustic mind was awed by preparations. On the night of the concert Desborough, who was the son of a man of independent means, strolled in and took a seat on one of the front benches. Chairs had been pressed into the service from all over the town, and the platform, with its decorations, was a fine imaginative effort. The Squire was there, and Sir John, the county member, brought his wife and her diamonds. After the imposing musician had conducted one or two glees, there was a little rustle of preparation, and a girl stepped forth to sing. To the tradesmen of the town she was simply Polly Blanch-flower, but to the thinking of one young man, who sat within a few yards of her, she ought to have been throned among stars. He had mixed little in company, and from the first time that the girl's eyes fell upon him he was a changed man.

She sang the " Flowers of the Forest." Where she had learnt her art I do not know, and the imposing musician from London could not guess. As she sang, Desborough fancied he could hear the cry of bereaved women. When the last verse came, the singer seemed to harden her voice to a martial tone, and the young man felt as though he must rise to his feet. As the last sound died, the great musician himself stepped forward and escorted the girl to the improvised seat at the rear of the platform. The audience had heard nothing of the kind before.

They did not think Mrs. Blanchflower's girl could work musical miracles. They clamoured until the singer came forward and sang them, " What's a the steer, Kimmer ? " and she finished the song with triumphant archness. In the interval between the first and the second part of the concert, Sir John imperatively demanded that the young lady should be brought to him, and he grumbled out words of approval which he considered very valuable.

Desborough went home and sat thinking hour after hour. His table was covered with papers. He looked at one sheet of manuscript and said, "What a fool I must have been to think that I could write! I have never begun to live until now. I will burn this last chapter and open a new one."

The other young men who had heard the songs were pleased, but they soon forgot, and thought only of Miss Blanchflower as a pretty girl who had a nice voice. Desborough was weak. His passion took complete command of him, and he was ready for any of those things that mad lovers do, and that staid people find so incredible. Within a month he had managed to meet the girl. Within two months she had learned that he was her slave. With the intuition that the most commonplace girls possess, she saw that he was never the man to be master, and she amused herself with him. The acquaintance ripened as the summer came on, and before the autumn the young fellow was ready to fetch and carry for his idol, and had surrendered his soul to her with tragic completeness.

There is something a little gross in this descent into slavery, but poor Desborough did not see it, for he was not given to self-introspection. He only knew that he was happy. A word exalted him, and he never felt a rebuff.

Miss Blanchflower's mother was a commonplace woman, who looked with a business eye upon the odd courtship that was passing in her household day after day. One evening she said to her daughter, "Marion, had not you better settle matters one way or the other?" The girl needed no explanation of particulars. She very well knew what were the matters referred to. She tossed her head and quietly replied, "Not with him, mother. When I marry a man, I marry my master. I like that poor fellow well enough. He looks nice and he talks prettily, but I always associate him with a poodle."

"But don't you think a man had better use his knees to kneel to you than use them to walk away from you?"

The girl said no more. Her mother had told her Desborough's income, and she knew that to break off the connection would bring about an ugly family quarrel.

On the very next night after this conversation Desborough called as usual, and began the ordinary pleasant and trifling gossip with which the simple people passed the evenings. Towards nine o'clock the mother rose.

"I shall have to leave you for about half an hour," she said, and the girl at once knew that that half hour was meant for decision. A few awkward minutes passed, and then Desborough made up his mind to speak. "I won't hint, and I won't spend time in words with you, Marion. You know all that I could say, and I should only vulgarize love if I talked."

The girl replied very quietly, "Well, we will take that as understood," and gave him her hand.

She liked him at that moment.

Everybody in the town had known what was coming, and the engagement was taken as a matter of course. When things had gone too far to allow of drawing back, Miss Blanchflower set herself to act a part. She did not really care for the man to whom she was engaged. In her heart she despised him a little, yet her artistic instinct allowed her to play at being in love, and she carried the comedy through with dexterity. The unequal companionship grew closer and closer, and Desborough was drawn deeper and deeper into forgetting himself, and forgetting all finer ambitions. He only sought to please the creature to whom he was slave, and the recognition which the girl now gave him made his happiness too deep for words.

But all the time Miss Blanchflower was weary. She cared for gaiety, and Desborough's mind was of a sombre cast; her artistic temperament made her sensuous, and Desborough's reserve was almost forbidding. He never spoke out, and the girl, who was always longing for violence of sentiment and sudden changes of emotion, found herself condemned to a dull, level life. Desborough would talk to her about poetry, but their tastes did not agree. He would even tease her with futile metaphysical talk until she scarcely knew whether to laugh or to flout him.

Another winter wore on, and the time for the wedding drew near. It happened that in the Spring a ball was given on the eve of a general election. A quarter of a mile of carriages stood in front of the Town Hall, and the county gentry mingled on terms of affability with the tradespeople and farmers of the

neighbourhood.   Desborough and Miss Blanchflower
were there, and the girl was strangely attractive, in
spite of her somewhat faulty taste in dress.   She gave
Desborough one dance, and spent the rest of the
evening in distributing favours.   A quiet conversation
passed in one corner of the room which would have
interested Miss Blanchflower very much could she
have heard.   Two men were standing together.   One
was a young fellow of about twenty-five.   He was
unspeakably slim, yet he carried himself with an air of
lithe strength.   His face looked as though it were
carven out of steel, so smooth and clean cut were his
features.   His hair was of unfashionable length, and
his dress was negligent, and yet no one could have
mistaken him for anything but a man of high breeding.
His eyes were brown, and had that velvety texture
of the iris which one sometimes sees amongst the
women of the New Forest, and sometimes among the
girls of the district round Bordeaux.   His whole
appearance was feminine, and the unstable glance that
he flashed from side to side spoke of vanity.   He said
to his companion, " Who is the prim virgin with the
fair hair ? "

" She is the daughter of a widow in the town.
Blanchflower, I think the name is."

" Do you think you could contrive an introduction ?
There is a sort of savage innocence about that dress
which rather attracts me."

Within half an hour Miss Blanchflower was con-
versing easily with the slim young gentleman who had
criticized her so pleasantly.

The girl was pleased to find this young fellow, who

was a sort of literary celebrity in his way, talking to her on equal terms. When he proposed a stroll in the improvised conservatory after the next dance, she was glad, although she felt that Desborough must be ill pleased.

When the last of the carriages had rolled away, and when the Town Hall was darkened, Marion Blanchflower was still sitting and thinking about the slim young man. Desborough was forgotten, and the girl only had thoughts of this new acquaiutance who suggested to her mind nothing but vivacity, and colour, and brilliant life. In four days from that time Miss Blanchflower was strolling down a deep hollow which was known as the Dene.

The whole place was ablaze with hyacinths. Far as one could see along the deep cliff, where the murmuring stream had carved itself a bed, the flowers spread like sheets of blue fire. ·In the more distant hollows the delicate masses of colour lay like clouds of gorgeous mist. Shooting straight up from the beds of hyacinths, tall elms met overhead, and the rooks kept up a clamour that dulled the senses without causing anything like irritation. The girl stepped down the path, and the light from the green leaves floated around her and touched her face and figure with delicate shadows and flickering brightness. She looked a joyous and beautiful creature, and the slim young man who met her by accident thought that he had never seen any picture so full of youth and delight.

The meeting was a pure coincidence.

The days passed on, and again and again Miss

M

Blanchflower walked in the Dene amid the flame of the hyacinths. Her mother trusted her greatly, and Desborough was too simple to have any afterthought when he found that his morning visits were discouraged. He was grateful for every moment of her company, and he placidly looked forward to the time when his quiet life should be crowned. Sometimes he chatted quite contentedly with Mrs. Blanchflower until Marion returned. Several people in the town could have told him things that would have surprised him, but he held so much aloof from all company that nobody ventured on familiar talk with him. The one man who had his confidence was the Wesleyan local preacher; but Musgrave lived a long way from the town, and Desborough saw him seldom.

One morning Desborough went down by the end of the stream. The water was low, and underneath the roots of a great tree there was a deep hollow that had been scooped out by the torrents of winter. An odd fancy made Desborough climb down and creep into this cavity under the network of roots. From the place where he was seated he could not only see the clear water running away seaward, but he could look right up the path that ran among the tall elms.

He was gazing mechanically on the ripples, and had allowed his mind to be hushed into complete vacuity by the delicate babble of the water over the pebbles, when suddenly a flash of colour seemed to grow upon his consciousness, and he saw a man and woman walking together down the very path that led to the cave where he had been dreaming. He placed his hand to his forehead and tried to think. It seemed as though his heart had been touched with ice. He would have called out, but he was stupefied. After a few long minutes he saw Miss Blanchflower make a sudden movement and give both her hands to her companion. The two stood face to face, and seemed to be speaking passionately. Desborough covered his eyes, and would see no more.

How long he sat he never knew; but when he was able to realize his place and to realize the fact of existence, he was alone. He moaned, and then by one of those revolutions of feeling common to men of his temperament, he broke into laughter.

As he climbed out from his retreat his sense of the tragic turn of things left him, and he laughed still more.

"And I am an eaves-dropper, am I? Mr. Hamlet Desborough. And Ophelia's not talking to her father this time. What a nice young Polonius we have got—ambrosial curls Polonius has—And Ophelia! Oh! Ophelia's very fair—chaste as an icicle, and pure as snow."

He walked towards a deep pool that lay further down towards the sea. The pool was very sullen and cool under the dank shadow of the hanging trees. Desborough looked a minute into the dark depths.

"Now, Hamlet, let us finish up. Let me see. What are the puzzles that I have to solve? Death? That's soon done. Three minutes, they say, it takes under water. And that other country where the travellers go and never return? Well, I don't see particularly why I should return, and oh! Ophelia, Ophelia."

He sat down and looked at the water until gradually his impulse wore off, and his face grew stern. He muttered no more as he walked home; he passed people in the street, but made no sign; he had revenge, fear, rage, pity, and love in his heart, and his passions were too strong for his will. Had he not been able to gain solitude there is no knowing what he might have done, for no man does such terrible things, and no man is so utterly reckless as a thoroughly weak individual who is suddenly cast adrift from all his mental holdfasts.

Before night he had written a little note. These were the words that he wrote :—

" My· dearest, I have been thinking bad thoughts of you all day. Now I have come to myself. I know where you were this morning, and I know that my life is broken. I will not thrust my claim upon you, and I cannot ask you for pity. You will not see me again. I give you up without one reproach. I only reproach myself for wearying you, and for trying to entrap you into a life that would have been misery to you. I was meant for a failure ; I was meant to pass through the world unknown and unheeded, saving by those near to me. You require larger interests. I am glad I have loved you, I am sorry I led you into treachery. Good-bye."

The town's folk missed Desborough for a long while after this, and then it gradually oozed out that he had broken off his engagement. Anyone who knows what the gossip of a provincial town is like, will understand the wrath and indignation that followed this proceeding. Poor Desborough fancied he had been sacrificing himself, and, if the truth must be told, felt a little proud of his own nobility. Yet all the while many tongues were tearing his reputation to shreds.

He had come to London, thinking the rush and hurry of crowded life would brighten his thoughts, and he was walking dreamily down the turbulent Strand one evening when he met a man from his own town. He stepped up to his acquaintance and stopped. The man looked him in the face and passed on. Desborough turned and walked alongside, saying with quick breathing, " Why do you refuse me your hand ? I have not seen a face I know for days, weeks—I don't know how long."

The man replied, " Look here, Desborough, I don't like cutting any fellow, but I wish you had not tried to speak to me."

" What do you mean ? "

" It is very shabby of you to ask what I mean. I do not pretend to be a saint at all, but there are things no fellow can stand. I wish you would let me say good day."

" But I insist upon knowing."

" Knowing what ? You know what you have done, and I should think that ought to be enough to serve you. I shall tell you nothing more."

" Turn down into one of the quiet streets, and for pity's sake tell me what you mean."

They walked into the Adelphi, and Desborough's friend said, " I thought you had a bit of the man about you. Why do you thrust yourself on me ? You pretend to know nothing about the girl, and I call it shabby, there now ! "

Presently Desborough found himself standing alone.

The whole position flashed upon him. He could not go back. He saw that his character was gone, and he saw that he was blamed for destroying a character that he had held more precious than his own. He went to his chambers and wrote to a relation for money. He intended to sell all that he owned, and he simply asked for an advance so that he might get out of the country quickly, and place the greatest possible distance between himself and his home before he finally parted with all that belonged to him. He waited for two days, and the reply came :—

" Referring to your letter of the 20th, I beg to state that I cannot do what you wish. I am sorry that you have been in any way connected with me, and I can only ask you now not to remind me of an intimacy and of a relationship which I have cause to consider disgraceful. Your name is mixed with the worst scandal that we have had in the town for years. The girl would not speak a word against you, but her mother has said enough."

The same relation furnished Desborough's address to Mrs. Blanchflower, and a letter from the lady reached him: "I have no reproaches to make, excepting that I am sorry you should think that we would pursue you."

Desborough wrote back : " I cannot do more than guess the accusation you lay against me. I acted as I thought was best, and I give you my word that I would die before hurting you or yours. I have a suspicion of the real cause of your cruel letter, and the suspicion almost kills me. I cannot come back to mix myself with the sordid scandal, and I can only say that, whatever you may think of me, I deserve nothing but your kindest thoughts."

His innocent precipitancy had involved the poor fellow in a web which he had not nerve or insight enough to break. He saw that the woman he loved had allowed an accusation to be laid against him, and he saw that she wanted to shield her real lover, yet he would not baulk her by clearing himself.

How he spent the next year of his life it would be useless to tell. At first he drank, but the blank misery that follows the wretched exaltation of drunkenness was too much for him, and he tried no more to seek relief that way. It was then said that he tramped the country for many months, and that he worked as a common blacksmith with a man who travelled the roads in Cheshire. Then one of his letters bore the post-mark of a small Norman town, and so from time to time rumours of him reached the place where his name was mentioned with anger by women and contempt by men.

Marion Blanchflower died, and the news of her death reached Desborough by the merest chance while he was prosecuting one of his aimless journeys among the hamlets of the Black Forest. But it was then too late for him to go back. For ten years all news of him ceased. He never told anyone what he had done during these years of his life. One after another the people who had known him in the old town died off, and when, at last, an impulse that he could not restrain forced him to see the place where his happiness had blossomed and died, no one knew that the bent figure with grizzled hair was that of Desborough.

The same indecision prompted him at last to hire the old cottage that stood on our moor, and thus it was that I came to see him.

A year afterwards I heard Desborough speak some very simple and touching words to a rough audience of fishermen. The gnarled faces looked placid as the clever, broken man talked on, and Desborough's own face seemed to have grown spiritual. His eye had an expression of quiet sadness, but I liked him better as a preacher than as a philosopher.

He seemed to be happier too, and before death came on him, like a summer night falling over the stress of daytime, he had become very reverend, and very lovable.

MR. CASELY.

I.

YOUNG Mr. Ellington strolled down the narrow walk that led through the woods from the Hall to the sea. The morning had lain heavy on his hands, for he was without companionship, and he was not one of the happy folk who can make resources or who find a sufficient delight in mere living. A few sharp commonplaces delivered with dry imperiousness by the old Squire; a little well-meaning babble from a couple of timid maiden aunts — such was the range of his converse with his kind from day to day. And this quiet dreariness had lasted for months past, and seemed likely to last so far into the future that young Ellington faced his prospect with a sort of pained confusion of mind, and began by slow degrees to understand the bovine apathy of the ploughmen. Old Mr. Ellington was a magnate who would have been commended by Mr. John Ruskin. The fashions of other country people did not influence him to imitation, and he steadfastly performed that feat of " living on the land " which is supposed to bring such blessedness to all whom the land supports. For fifty years he had never been twenty miles beyond the bounds of his

southernmost farm, and for fifty years the ugly Hall
had never opened its doors to an invited guest.
People talked a good deal, and made theories more or
less malignant, but the hard old man minded them no
whit. He went on his own road with perfect propriety,
outraging every convention in the most virtuous
manner, and opposing a dry reticence to the curiosity
and wonderment of the few neighbours who continued
to have any vivid remembrance of his existence. In
fine weather his stout and opinionated cob bore him
gravely along the lanes. The cottagers' children ceased
their play and looked respectfully sheepish as he rode
by ; the farm girls dropped their elaborate curtseys,
and the labourers at the roadside made efforts to appear
at their ease. These and the farmers were the only
people who saw his daily progress, and they all held
him a good deal in fear. Nothing escaped his steady
eye. If anything displeased him he did not use words,
for he had not talents of the vocal description, but he
took very sudden means of making his displeasure felt.
Within his domain he was absolute master. He disliked the intrusion of even passing strangers, and the
harmless bagmen who sometimes travelled along the
coast road found no hostelry on the estate. It was
said that he once met an alien person walking in the
woods, and that this erratic foreigner was smoking a
pipe. The most learned purveyors of myths were
never able to detail exactly what happened, but the
incident was always mentioned with awe. The inhabitants of the district never managed to get up
any personal feeling about the Squire ;—they regarded him as an operation of Nature. So he lived

his life in his colourless fashion, rousing no hate,
gaining no love, and fulfilling his duties as though his
own epitaph were an abiding vision to him. He cared
for no enjoyments, and did not particularly like to see
other people enjoying themselves. He seemed to fancy
that laughter should be taken like the Sacrament, and,
for his own part, he preferred not being a communicant.
When his only son was killed in a pitiful frontier
skirmish, the old man rode out as usual on the day
following the receipt of the ill news. The gamekeeper
said that he drew up his cob alongside the fence of a
paddock wherein was kept an aged pony that the heir
had ridden long ago. He watched the stumbling
pensioner cropping the bright grass for a few minutes,
breathed heavily, turned the cob into the road again,
and went on with sharp eyes glancing emotionless.
His daughter-in-law died soon after, and he assumed
sole charge of the young Ellington whom we have seen
making a forlorn pilgrimage under the trees. The
young man had received a queer sort of nondescript
education. All the Ellingtons for a generation or two
back had gone in due course to Eton and Oxford, but
no such conventional training was vouchsafed to the
latest of the family. The hand of the private tutor
had been heavy upon him, and he was brought up
absolutely without a notion of what his own future
might be. He had mooned about among books to
some trifling extent, but the taste for study had never
taken him. The silly mode of culture which he had
undergone availed nothing against the instincts of his
race. His grandfather was a sort of living aberration
—a queer variety such as Nature will sometimes inter-

polate amid the most steady of strains; but young Ellington's moods, and tendencies, and capabilities reverted to the old line. Yet, despite his restless energy, despite his incapacity for that active thought which makes solitude bearable, he was crushed into the mould that the Squire had prepared for him. His distractions were few, and in his vigorous mind, with its longing for instant action, its continual revolt against self-contained speculation, there arose a dull fear of the future, a longing for deliverance. It was not a merry existence for a young man who heard the brave currents of life sounding around him and calling him vaguely to come and adventure himself with the rest. He knew that the sons of the men who laughed at his grandfather laughed also at him, and regarded him with a somewhat impertinent wonder, but he dared explain himself to none, and dared seek companionship with none. This is why he looked so listless as he lounged toward the sea that fine afternoon. There was enough all round him to please anyone with an eye for the quiet beauty of inanimate things. The lights slid and quivered on the golden windings of the walk. Here and there the beams that came through were toned into a kind of floating greenness that looked glad and tender. The light wind overhead set the leaves talking, and their silky rustle sounded sharp through the low murmur of the near sea. Now and then came other sounds. A cushat would moan from her high fir-top, or a pheasant deep in the shadows would call with his resonant guttural. But young Mr. Ellington did not heed the sounds and sights that asked his attention; he hardly heeded his own being, and his footsteps grated on till the veil of the trees seemed drawn back, and he saw the shining sea glimmering under a light haze. Far out toward the centre of the blue circle, a fishing-boat lunged heavily as the deliberate rollers came shoreward, and upon this boat he fixed his eye with that meaningless intentness born of weariness.

He had begun to time his vague thought by the regular swing of the black boat, when his attention was called by a clinking sound. Someone was trying to open a wicket which opened from a by-road to the left of him. He caught a glimpse of bright colour through the bars, and stepped smartly forward. The wicket was easy to open from his side, and he soon released the wayfarer from trouble. She took one slight pace back, curtsied, and said, " Thank you, sir." It was not a very remarkable speech, but coming upon Ellington's ear in his blank mood, it sounded friendly and pleasant to a strange degree. He wanted to hear the voice again. He rested for a brief space—not long enough to make the interval seem awkward—and glanced swiftly at the girl whom he had aided. His faculties did not rise readily into keenness after his recent hour of lethargy, but he saw in an indefinite way that she was tall, and the elastic pose of her figure as she prepared to pass by him gave him somehow an impression of power. After an instant of hesitation he met the clear look of a pair of brown eyes, and he felt that he must say something. He fancied his slight pause had made him appear a trifle clumsy, and he. sought to effect a graceful parting. But, alas ! for the grace of solitary young men ! The one right phrase, the one right gesture would not come, and so, although his manner was sufficiently easy at ordinary times, he could only say, "I'm very glad I happened to be by." The girl was not sophisticated enough to regard him with anything like humour. She smilingly accepted his remark as cogent, and replied, "Yes. Old Trumbull has funny notions about fitting on latches, hasn't he?" Here was a distinct opportunity for further pleasing conversation, and the unfortunate Mr. Ellington was feeble. "Oh, you know Trumbull?" he said, with alacrity. "He and I are great friends, but I don't interfere with his professional matters. I'm afraid he would discharge me if I did."

This was an unmistakably humorous allusion, and the girl once more flashed her white teeth in a pretty smile. Such a reception of his not very striking remarks put the young man at his ease, and he became composed enough to observe delicately the face of his new acquaintance. He had but little time, for of course he could not stand for long babbling stupidities with a country girl. The face was strong and dark, with composed, full lips, and a dusky glow in the cheeks. The eyes which had at first put him to such confusion looked liquid and strangely attractive when the light of laughter was in them. Mr. Ellington had fallen in with a beautiful girl. He did not formulate any opinion on the subject all at once, but he prolonged the conversation into the second five minutes. Then he said casually, "I've not seen you passing this way before," and the dark young lady made answer, with complete simplicity, "No, but I always come through here on Thursday afternoons as I go to my aunt's over at the Dean."

Mr. Ellington said "good-bye" at last, and the tall, strong figure of the girl disappeared round a bluff of the shrubbery, her feet lighting on the gravel with crisp, decided firmness.

It was not an exciting incident, but in truth the things that alter lives, and give us our strongest emotions, do really happen in fashions the reverse of picturesque. A couple of young folk had exchanged a score or so of vapid words, yet before many weeks had gone several people had reason for wishing the trivial interview had never been.

The girl thought but once more about the matter. On her way back the clink of the closing wicket brought young Ellington to her mind again, and she said to herself, "What a nice free lad the young squire is! They were saying he was a kind of close fellow with a bad temper. He doesn't look like that. I wonder what makes him flatten his hair down so funny? He asked me about next Thursday." And there Miss Mary Casely ceased her maiden meditations, and walked on with her sharp step, and with a mind vacant of all coherent thought, as only the truly rustic mind can be. Presently she passed a row of one-storied cottages which ran along the edge of the low cliff, and she tapped at the door of a somewhat larger house which stood in a dignified manner a little apart from the fishermen's cottages. She heard a strong voice say, "Oh! It's her, back again." Then a heavy step crunched the sand of the flooring, and made the windows rattle in their frames. The door opened, and the same deep voice said, "Ye've getten here then, hinny. What kind of a night is it?"

The man stooped low to escape the lintel, and then straightened himself up in the road.

If you had searched from Yarmouth to Berwick the whole coast along you could not have found a more superb creature. He stood six feet four, but his limbs were so massive, and the outward arch of his broad chest was so full, that you might easily have guessed his inches wrongly. As he turned westward toward the last light that still glowed in dim bars from behind the hills, his face showed with a noble outline. He looked round for a space, said, "Ay, the lads'll be having a bonny night," then strode heavily to his "settle" once more, and prepared to chat with his daughter. When the lamp was lit, the grandeur of his face became finely apparent. His hair was coarse, and black, and lustreless; it hung heavily over a heavy brow. His jaw was square and powerful, but its firmness was saved from seeming absolutely cruel by the kindly lines of the mouth. Not a feature of the man was unmarked by signs of keenness and strength. You would not have chosen him for an enemy unless you happened to be a thought inexperienced. This was Mr. Thomas Casely. For fifty-four years he had dwelt in that house on the cliff-edge; his father still lived in one of the small cottages near by, and his grandfather and great-grandfather had spent their lives in the same village before him. Probably the progenitors of the Caselys and the Ellingtons came over together on a thieving expedition, and, finding the natives of the region amenable to emphatic arguments, settled quietly and used their long vessels henceforth for comparatively honest purposes.

A deal of very curious talk is spent over the ancient Scandinavians who used to harry the peaceful farmers long ago. We learn that these rapacious gentlemen were above all things "deep-thoughted," and that they had rather fine notions about poetry and the future life. They were, in short, a species of blood-thirsty Æsthetics. Instead of devoting themselves to intense amours and sonnets, they were the Don Juans of Death, but in no other point did they differ materially from the cultured creature who lives up to his blue china.

This notion seems wrong. From all observations, I should incline to say that the earliest Ellington who settled in England was a big ruffian who disliked work, and who had a sharp eye to business ; whilst the earliest Caselys were probably thievish fellows, who loved moonless nights, and objected to the use of cold water. Under the influence of softening generations, the Caselys and Ellingtons had dropped their predatory tendencies, and lived peaceful lives. Furthermore, it is certain that the heartiest amity had prevailed between the houses for more years than I care to reckon. Travel and town life had given polish to some of the aristocrats, and taught them to use reasonable haughtiness toward inferior creatures ; but even a haughty greeting is better than a remonstrance delivered with a mace. At any rate, all the Caselys were brought up to offer reverence to the Squire, and the tradition of mutual esteem and distant respect had never been broken. A correct notion of the rights of labour had not been expounded anywhere near the estate, and the roughest fellow on Mr. Ellington's land

N

probably felt loyalty towards the Family. This state
of things cannot withstand the advance of culture for
very long, but meantime it offers even unto this day
an interesting specimen of ancient usage.

When his daughter had got out her knitting, Thomas
Casely drew down his shaggy brows, and looked at
her with a queer twinkle of kindness.

" You'll have had a grand talk with them over at the
Dean ? "

" No, father.   The old Squire rode round, and he
wanted to see so many things about the stackyard,
aunt couldn't get away.   Bob was in for a minute."

" What for didn't Bob see you home ? "

" Oh, I cannot be fashed with him.   When he's
dressed to come out, he looks just like as if he'd got
mixed suits of other folks' clothes on."

" You'll not have to be proud, my woman.   He's
just as good, and better, than the most of the lads
round here.   I never knew no good come of pride."

" I never knew what pride meant; but if I walk
with a lad I like him to be bonny, and I want to see
him not look like a countryman altogether.   Bob isn't
bonny."

" Ay, well, hinny, if you want fine clothes, I doubt
you'll get nobody but the young squire."   This Mr.
Casely said with a slow smile, and Mary thought suddenly, " Next Thursday afternoon."

The reader will see that these rustics had not attained
that quaint sententious wisdom proper to the rustics of
fiction.   In their ungrammatical way they talked much
like human beings.

II.

WHEN Mr. Ellington turned once more to the sea, after Mary Casely had passed out of sight, the look of things had somehow altered in his eyes. He went to the edge of the rocks, and looked down on the short ripples that broke into whiteness below him. He was taken with the beauty of the clear green water that moved over the shallows, and he found himself watching the swift changes of shade caused by the passage of the light breeze with something like active interest. The ragworts and the wild geraniums made a yellow and purple fretwork all around him, and the colour gave him a sense of keen gladness. He faced round and entered the quivering gloom of the woods again, but his step on the gravel was sharp and firm. Every faculty of him seemed to have waked. A blackbird bugled cheerily in the underwood, and Ellington felt a strange thrill. He reached the Hall, and sat down to wait for the dressing-bell, but the hour before dinner, usually so heavy to him, went by briskly. During dinner he made no attempt at sustained conversation, yet he answered his grandfather's few short questions with a ready cheerfulness and fluency which made the old man regard him with narrowed eyes.

When the night came fairly on, he sat looking out of his window into the scented darkness. Had you asked him what he was thinking of, he could not have told you, yet I suppose something unusual must have been passing through his mind, for, when he had

finally risen with a sigh of content to close the window,
he stepped up to the looking-glass and regarded himself with curiosity.   Once he smiled, as if by way of
practice, and then a sudden sense of shame seemed
to come over him, for he reddened and turned away.
Most people will be able to guess what ailed him, but
he himself did not know at the time.

The week went away but slowly.   On the Wednesday
evening the old Squire said : "You'll go over to
Branspath to-morrow morning early.   Richards will
drive you in, and you must call on Chernside and tell
him I wish to see him in the afternoon about Gibson's
lease.   He'll know what you mean."   The young man
shifted uneasily.   "Couldn't you send a note by
Richards?"   He felt his face hot as he asked the
question.

"Well, yes, I could, if I chose, but I want Richards
to order a few things in the High Street.   He'll pick
you up when you've done with Chernside."   At two
o'clock next day young Mr. Ellington was back again
at the Hall.   As he stepped down from the dog-cart,
Richards pointed to the horse.   "I doubt we've done
him some harm, Sir.   Forty-five minutes from the
High Moor—the black mare couldn't do it no quicker.
Matchem here hasn't been driven for three weeks now."
The horse was drooping his head, the lather slid down
his flanks,—so I fancy there had been hard going.

The young Squire gave an indifferent look and
hurried indoors.   Within an hour he was walking
rather quickly toward the sea, without one sign of
the dreaminess that overweighed him when last he
took the same road.   Presently (he knew it would come)

a firm step came over the gravel, and his heart went fast. Before he had got rid of his momentary dimness of sight, he found himself obliged to stammer out something : "You managed the wicket by yourself this time." The girl laughed brightly. Ellington felt bound to go on speaking—

"You are going over to the Dene ?"

"Yes; I think I'll take the short cut through the Ride."

"I think, if you don't mind, we may as well go by the Three Plantations." He said "we" with the utmost ease, and, noticing no sign of dissent, he walked on by the side of the girl, and a new chapter of his life began.

Neither of them could tell exactly how they came to be walking together, yet each of them would have been disappointed had it not fallen out so. Neither of them had made a definite resolve to meet the other, but the girl had made most calculations on the event. Within a month from that day the pair were strolling under the gloom of the firs in the Three Plantations. This time young Mr. Ellington had his arm round his companion's waist; her tall figure was leaned towards him.

They were talking low, and the rustling sound of their whispers echoed a little beneath the sombre arch of the trees.

They came to the little bridge which crossed the head of the Dean, and then he took both her hands and said, "Now, good-bye; to-morrow at the high end of the New Plantation." They had got to daily meetings within that short month.

"I'll be there. You won't mind if I'm a bit behind time? Sometimes they want me, and I don't care for my father to ask where I'm going."

"I've promised to wait for you, darling, half a lifetime, if need be. Why should I grudge an hour?"

This question was not articulately answered, but the reply was satisfactory. Then the couple parted.

So it happened that in a few brief weeks this quiet young man had drifted into a disgraceful intrigue. He did not think it disgraceful, because he had not reflected at all. The future was barred to him, and he lived from one day to another content with the joy that the day brought. He had made promises with rash profusion, and his promises had been believed. Further and further he had been drawn, till the fire of his blood made him fancy that he was proceeding voluntarily.

To Mary Casely the whole affair seemed quite natural. She knew nothing about the pitiful stories of village maidens which make so much of the stock of fiction. She had never read a story, so she fancied that her secret meetings were part of the fixed order of life. She happened to have a sweetheart who dressed well and spoke beautifully, and that was all the difference between her and other girls. Besides this, she was a singularly determined young woman. She had made up her mind to marry the young Squire; he in his folly had given no single hint of the vast, the insuperable difficulties that lay in the way; and so the bitter business went on.

The summer passed into autumn, and late November came. Such an affair as that of Mary Casely and the young Squire could not be long kept out of the reach

of acrid village gossip. Once or twice, as young
Ellington walked out of church from the pew by the
chancel, he fancied he saw the gardeners and farm-
people looking at him with intelligence, and he felt
something catching at his throat.

When December came in, his misery had grown to
acuteness. His old passive wretchedness had given
way to a settled nervous dread which wore the brightness from his comely face.

One grey afternoon he took the old road to the sea
again. The wind was crying drearily, and the trees
creaked as they swayed to each swift gust. He
shivered when he came in sight of the sea, for the low
sky was leaden. The very foam looked dull. Every
few seconds came a muffled boom, as a roller shattered
itself against the rocks, and a tower of spray shot up
and fell on the sodden grass.

The wild flowers were gone, and the bents bowed
themselves cheerlessly.

How many things else were gone ! How many things
else were cheerless !

He turned round when he could bear waiting no longer,
and prepared to carry his miseries home. Something
ill must have happened. At the bluff of the shrubbery
where he had first seen Mary pass out of sight he heard
a step, but it was not that sharp, steady step he had
learnt to know so well. He was face to face with Mr.
Casely. It had come at last. For weeks he had fore-
shadowed this meeting in his dreams, and the fear had
so worked on him that he had learned a trick of glancing
suddenly over his shoulder. Casely looked steadily
down at the young Squire for a time that seemed

long, and then, unclenching his tense jaw, said quietly—

"It wasn't me you were expecting to meet."

"I didn't expect to meet you. No; how do you come to be passing this way?"

"I've been up to the Hall seeing your grandfather. You know what I've been for very near as well as I do. And now I have to talk to you. Speak straight, or I'll break you in two across my knee."

Ellington was not more of a coward than other men. But he didn't heed the threat. His grandfather knew. Nothing else was in his stunned mind. He stood staring—unable to get a word past his lips. Casely spoke, louder—

"What ails you? Have I to hit you?"

Then the young fellow found his voice.

"I wish you would. I wish you would kill me where I stand. I'm all in the wrong, and I have no right to answer you. It began well—I mean, I meant no harm. Never any man dared offer one of us a blow before, but it has come to that now. I wouldn't lift a hand to stop you. I haven't an excuse to give you."

"A nice thing it is for your father's son to be standing slavering there and cowering to me like a whelp. I don't despise you for it, for I know what you mean; but isn't it bonny? You haven't an excuse! Have you nothing else—not a promise like them you've made to the lass?"

"I'd marry her now, but I know it would be a hundred thousand times worse for her than if she married a common sailor man. I'm past wretchedness. It couldn't be."

"And what about her? And, what about me? How is it for us? Now, look you, my fine young man! I'll not stop a minute longer, or else there'll be murder. But I'll tell you this much. I know as well as you there can be nothing more. I'm not mad. She can't marry you, and you knew that before you started lying to her. It's all over, and we must face the folk in the place the best way we can. You're sorry, I see you are; but understand this—sorry or not, if it wasn't that me and my forebears has had nothing but good from them that went before you, and was better than you, I'd kill you now, and reckon you no more than a herring. You'd better get away out of my sight."

Then Mr. Casely tramped towards the wicket, and went home. He sat long into the night, and when he went to bed he flung himself on the coverlid with his clothes on. Towards morning he said aloud—"I'm glad he didn't think to offer me money. If he had, I would have pulled his windpipe out."

The young gentleman thus alluded to by Mr. Casely had gone home in a state of stupefaction. He did not attempt to frame a thought. His limbs took him along mechanically. He passed one of his aunts as he went to his room, but he did not make any sign. When he had settled down, a tap came at his door.

"Mr. Ellington'll have dinner laid for him in his study. He wants to see you, Sir, in the study as soon after dinner as possible."

Young Ellington heard this without any fresh shock. The worst had passed, and nothing henceforth could hurt him.

He could eat nothing. He found himself adding up

the number of glasses; dividing it into couples; counting the squares on the wall-pattern; going through all the forlorn trivialities that employ the mind when suffering has passed out of the conscious stage. When his time came for meeting the terrible old man, he stepped straight into the study without knocking, and stood stupidly waiting for the voice that he knew would come. A thought of dignity never occurred to him. Had he been a mere libertine he would have brazened it out, and would have tried at flippancy. But he was not a libertine; he was simply an inexperienced young man who was suffering remorse at its deadliest.

"You had better sit down."

He sought a chair, took his seat, and once more waited.

"Need we exchange any words about this business? You can have nothing to say, so perhaps you had better leave the talking to me. You have behaved like a scoundrel. You have crippled my hands. Only a year ago I turned Thomson's girl off the estate, and gave her father notice to quit the cottage after her. I got some newspaper chatter aimed at me then, and now, by God, you've done worse than the fellow who ruined poor Thomson. Look up there, and you'll see your father's portrait. He was a merry lad in his day, but he wouldn't have intrigued with a washerwoman. That's about what you have done. However, we'll have no more scolding. Of course, you understand that the affair is to be done with?"

"It depends upon you, Sir. If you will, I dare marry her."

"I thought you were a little mad. Go! I wish I could say go for altogether. I have some time to live though, and you shall know something meanwhile. Go!"

The unfortunate had not a word to say even against his grandfather's brutal insolence. He went, and passed the night in much the same way as did Casely, save that where Casely's pride was still stubborn, Ellington's pride was broken.

III.

WHEN the spring came there were gay doings at the Hall. Old Mr. Ellington had taken a sudden turn, and the housekeeper was near bidding good-bye to her reason. There were extra men engaged in the stables, and the black mare, Matchem, and the Squire's cob had very grand company indeed. Things went so far that one morning the Branspath hounds met on the Common by the Hall. For fifty-five years such a thing had not been seen. The great dappled dogs stood in a clump by the high north wall of the fruit garden, and the villagers stared round in wonder. The gorse to the southward of the House was drawn, and a fox was found. There was a wild crash and clamour for a few minutes in the plantation where Mary Casely used to meet her lover, and then I am sorry to say that the Huntsman began to use very bad language. Nothing had been attended to; the hounds might as well have been entered at rabbits. The fox never even had occasion to break covert, and the gay assemblage rode away towards Branspath before two o'clock in the afternoon. The science of earth-stopping had not been pushed to its final term on the Ellington estate, but still there was hope now that the hounds had once been permitted to cross the border which divided Squire Ellington's property from that of the next sporting landowner.

After the abortive intrusion of the hounds there were still other attempts at gaiety. The village began somehow to look brisk; the ancient stagnation passed away, and grey cottagers spoke fondly of the old times.

Throughout all this liveliness Mr. Casely kept to the mode of living he had adopted ever since the night when he made allusions to Mr. Ellington's wind-pipe. He went about his work as usual, but he spoke to no one. He dropped going to church, and he never, as in past times, drove his cart into Branspath. Mary had been sent to a relation's in the South. Her father would not mention her name, and his family and neighbours were particularly careful to say nothing about the girl who had gone. Sometimes Casely would think about his pet, but he spared words. Once a neighbour stepped in unawares, and found the strong man stretched with his face on the settle, and sobbing hard; but he sat up when he found he was not alone, spoke an oath or two, and was ready for every-day chat.

In the autumn Casely happened to be out on the green, watching the women spreading the nets to dry. It was a lovely day, and the larks were singing wildly one against the other far up toward the sky. Suddenly the chattering women grew quiet. A slender young lady, daintily dressed, walked gracefully along the road that bordered the green. There was silence while she passed, save for the larks' sweet jargoning. As soon as the neat tall figure was sufficiently far off, one of the women said—

" Who's that ? "

Another made answer within Casely's hearing—

" Oh, it's the young Squire's lass. She's a daughter of some big man away down South. They're to be married come the spring o' the year."

Casely watched the graceful young lady over the crest of the next rise, then turned homeward and sat down silent as usual. Now it happened that the lady when she passed the gossiping fishers was going to meet young Ellington. That gentleman had lately persuaded his grandfather to buy a light boat for the better navigation of a heavy dull stream that ran deep and silent round the southerly border of the home farm, and the individual undutifully referred to as " the young Squire's lass " was about to trust herself in the new craft with her lover. Ellington had everything ready when the girl reached the stream. When she had stepped aboard, he said—

" You called at Marchman's for Aunt Esther and Miss Marshall ? "

" Yes! But they teased. They said they were having such an interesting gossip with poor old Hannah, they would prefer following me. They thought we might employ our time till they came up."

" It's just as well. I'm sure, if you don't mind, I don't. Which way shall we go ? "

"I cannot tell. The stream is so slack I could hardly guess where the sea lay if I didn't know."

"Well, now, I'll tell you what I propose doing. We can slip over the bar as the wind is just now. There's always a little rough water just where the burn joins the sea, but when we get over that the sea outside is quite smooth. Then we can sail, and save the bore of pulling."

So the confident young man pointed the boat's stem down stream, and after a little jerky work on the bar stood clear out into blue water.

He was used to sailing, so that he really took his boat rather cleverly round to the north-east. Then he made fast the sheet, since he wanted one hand free; the boat lay prettily over till the water gurgled again under her sharp bows, and Mr. Ellington felt the contentment and exhilaration born of swift movement. But of course he must needs proceed in this matter as in all others without thought of the future. The tide was running fast out, and a surface current which always skirts the bay set the boat ever more eastward. The rocks grew a little dim before Ellington looked round and considered the situation. He felt quite easy in his mind, however, and, stepping forward, let go the tiny halliard, whereupon the sail came down.

"Now," he said, "we're just going to let her take her own way for an hour."

This sailor-like resolution pleased his companion mightily, so the boat was allowed to wheel lazily, and curtsey to the slight waves as they set to the shore. Then the young people chatted softly, and forgot the time.

Now those who have watched the humours of autumn weather by the coast will have noticed that very often after a warm breeze has been blowing for hours, there will suddenly come a chill easterly waft. This will be followed by a steady cold wind. The trees are blown white, the grass is black with shadows, and the sea springs up like magic into a short nasty "lipper." Within half-an-hour the lipper has gathered size, and in a terribly short time there are ugly, medium-sized waves bowling fiercely and regularly westward. The change mostly comes just about an hour after the tide has turned. Ellington and his companion were talking on heedlessly, when the girl, interrupting him in the middle of a speech, said, shivering, "How cold it has turned!"

"Yes," returned Ellington, "it often comes like that. Do you see how she's beginning to caper? So, there! Softly, softly!" he cried, as though he were talking to a horse. A spirt of water had jerked over the boat's side.

He ran up his sail, and as the little craft swung on her light heels, and drew away to the west, he said, "I wish I hadn't got you into this mess. But never mind, I don't think it's more than a wetting and a fuss when we get home, at the worst of it."

Mr. Casely was sitting by his fire in the sanded kitchen. Excepting two very old fellows, he was the only man left in the village that afternoon, for all the other men and lads had gone north on the morning tide. His noble face had got the beginnings of a few new lines since we first saw him; his mouth was sorrowful, and his brows fell heavier than ever.

A woman came in rather hurriedly, and said, " Thou'd better come out a minute, honey. The sea's come on very coarse, and the young Squire's boat's gettin' badly used out there, about a mile to the east'ard."

" Who's in her ? "

" The young Squire and his lass."

" I'll be out directly. Has he ever made the landin' before ? "

" Yes, but Tom's Harry was always with him."

When Casely stepped to the cliff edge, he saw that matters were a little awkward. The boat was as yet in no very great danger, but the real pinch would not come till Ellington tried to land. For two miles along the coast there was not a single yard of shore where you dared beach a boat, excepting just opposite the village. Here there was a broad gap through the jagged reef which fringed the shore, and through this gap the fishermen's boats had shot in fair or foul weather for more generations than men could remember.

Casely said to one of the women—

" He'll be all right if he comes in to the north of the Cobbler. If he doesn't, it's a bad job."

The Cobbler's Seat was one of a pair of huge rocks, which lay right in the very gap wherethrough the boats had to run in. A progressive people would have had the impediments blasted away, but the fisher-folk were above all things conservative, and so the Cobbler remained year after year to make the inward passage exciting. When the tide was running in hard, a boat attempting the south passage was certain to be taken

in a nasty swirling eddy, and dashed heavily against
the big stone. When any sea was on, the run in
required much nicety of handling.

Ellington had been told long ago that he must keep
the church tower and the flagstaff in one if he wanted
to hit the gap fairly. He carried out his instruction
as well as he knew how.

The boat came dashingly in, flinging the spray
gallantly aside as she ducked and plunged in the short
sea.

Casely saw that Ellington was going wrong. For
an instant he had an ungenerous thought. "Should
I save him?" He shook himself as though he were
shaking off water, and sang out with all the strength
of his tremendous voice—"Hard down with it!" He
waved to the northward with passionate energy. But
it was too late. The boat staggered as the eddy hit
her, swerved sharp to starboard, and took in a great
plash of water, then she struck the Cobbler, and kept
repeating the blow with vicious, short bumps that
stove in her head. Ellington sprang out, and got
a foothold. He seized the girl, and dragged her
beside him. The boat turned clumsily over, and
swirled away past. Then the wrecked couple climbed
out of reach of the lunging waves, and stood breath-
less. Casely said, "That's a bad job, Jinny. The
Cobbler'll be covered half a fathom in forty minutes'
time."

· The woman he spoke to was his cousin. She said,
"Can he swim?"

"Him! The big baby! He never could do anything like a man since the day he was whelped. Old

John Ellington would have had the lass half-way
ashore by this time."

"Let him drown!" This unladylike speech came
from Jinny, who had been very fond of Mary Casely.

"No! no!" said Casely, frowning heavily, "I'll
not do that, Jinny. Tell Hannah to fetch a rope, and
call the other women. If we could only have got a coble
out it would have been all right, but there's nobody
to pull except a few daft wives and old Adam."

"What are you going to do?"

"I'll swim off, and you women folk can haul me in
with the lass. After that I'll maybe try for *him*."

Then this rare fellow had the rope fastened under
his armpits, flung off his sea-boots and his sleeve-
waistcoat, and struck off with a breast stroke that
made never a splash. The spray cut his face, the
lashing feathers on the tops of the waves half-blinded
him, but he held doggedly on, and presently hung on
to the bladderweed that fringed the Cobbler's Seat.
He climbed lightly up, and spoke to the girl.

"You'll lie quiet, my bonny woman, and don't
be frightened if you get a mouthful or two. Let me
have you under the arms, and look smart."

He waved and shouted, then let himself lightly
down into the sea, while the women ran up the beach
with the straining rope. When his feet ground in
the shallow water, he was bleeding at the mouth, but
he carried the girl past the foam.

"Take her up to our house, and send for Bella to
put her in bed. She's nigh done for. And now, my
lasses, give us that dry rope; this one's over stiff."

He struck off again, and was not long in getting to

the stone; but it was difficult work to climb up, for the wind was fairly whistling by this time, and the waves had got a heavy impetus. Ellington was blue with cold, and chattering at the teeth. He had cramped his fingers in a hole bored by the common mollusc, which honeycombs the rocks, and as he crouched he looked not particularly noble.

"Now, my man, there isn't much time, or else this would be a fine place for us to have a talk. I've saved your lass for you, and I wish you had done the same to mine for me. Now, come on; and mind, if you struggle, I'll fell you like a stirk."

Once more the women ran to the high end of the beach, and then Ellington was handed to them, limp and sick with sea water.

This was how Mr. Casely revenged himself.

CHISWICK PRESS :—C. WHITTINGHAM AND CO. TOOKS COURT, CHANCERY LANE.

www.ingramcontent.com/pod-product-compliance
Lightning Source LLC
Chambersburg PA
CBHW030832270326
41928CB00007B/1018